Teaching and Learning Communication, Language and Literacy

Ann Browne

P·C·P

Paul Chapman
Publishing

First published 2007

Paul Chapman Publishing
A SAGE Publications Company
1 Oliver's Yard
55 City Road
London EC1Y 1SP

SAGE Publications Inc
2455 Teller Road
Thousand Oaks, California 91320

SAGE Publications India Pvt Ltd
B1/I1 Mohan Cooperative Industrial Area
Mathura Road, Post Bag 7
New Delhi 110 044

Library of Congress Control Number: 2006934091

A catalogue record for this book is available from the British
Library

ISBN- 978-1-4129-0208-3
ISBN- 978-1-4129-0209-0 (pbk)

Typeset by Dorwyn, Wells, Somerset
Printed in Great Britain by Athenaeum Press, Gateshead, Tyne & Wear
Printed on paper from sustainable resources

Teaching and Learning Communication, Language and Literacy

Contents

About the author

Ann Browne is a senior lecturer in education at the University of East Anglia, Norwich, UK where she works with trainee and practising teachers. Before working in higher education she taught in a number of schools in Manchester and London. Throughout her career she has been primarily interested in language and literacy and the education of young children.

Acknowledgements

I would like to thank Marianne Lagrange for her patience and help during the writing of this book.

I am grateful to the many children, students and teachers that I have worked with. Their curiosity and endeavours have prompted me to reflect on and learn about the best ways of teaching young children.

In particular, I would like to thank the staff and children of Angel Road First School, Norwich, Davies Lane Primary School, Waltham Forest, and Hillside Primary School, Norwich who contributed some of the examples and illustrations which bring this book to life.

Introduction

Children in the Foundation Stage are embarking on their life in organized learning environments. They enter pre-school settings and reception classes with curiosity and anticipation. Adults who work with children at this early stage have a special part to play in introducing young children to communication, language and literacy. To fulfil this important role they need to understand how children learn, the subjects that are to be taught and how to bring these two elements together to provide young learners with a stimulating and developmentally appropriate curriculum.

In this book I have attempted to cover all these elements. The book begins with a chapter which examines how children learn, the importance of play as a context for learning and teaching strategies that are appropriate to help children acquire knowledge, understanding and positive attitudes to learning. It is against this backdrop that the chapters on speaking and listening, reading and writing should be read. The chapters that are concerned with the curriculum for communication, language and literacy contain sections on subject knowledge. This is intended to help practitioners to understand what it is they are planning for and teaching. They also contain an indication of how children's learning develops in each of these aspects and include examples of activities that can contribute to children's development. Teaching is part of the plan, teach, assess and evaluate cycle that contributes to effective learning, and so the book ends with chapters on assessment and planning.

Equal opportunities is an important issue throughout education but perhaps has a particular significance in the Foundation Stage where children are forming attitudes and opinions about themselves and the world they live in. Research suggests that attendance at pre-schools and nurseries tends to benefit children's educational success and can compensate for the inequalities in some children's lives. As communication, language and literacy are often seen as the basis for success in and out of school, topics related to equal opportunities are explored within this book.

This book has been written for anyone who wants to know more about how to contribute to young children's learning. I hope that it conveys some of the shared excitement and enjoyment that are possible as adults and children work together in the early years.

Ann Browne
August 2006

Chapter 1

Setting the scene for communication, language and literacy

Introduction

Each phase of schooling, the Foundation Stage, Key Stage 1, Key Stage 2, Key Stage 3 and Key Stage 4 has its own distinctive characteristics and concerns. Some of the defining characteristics of the Foundation Stage are explored in this chapter and they provide the background to the teaching and learning of communication, language and literacy.

The curriculum, learning, teaching and classroom organization are important concerns in every phase but they are realized in ways that are particular to the age and needs of the pupils. The curriculum for the Foundation Stage, although separated into areas of learning, reflects the way in which young children's learning rarely fits neatly into one area of the curriculum. In the Foundation Stage the boundaries between different subjects are blurred and even in a single activity learning can take place in a number of curriculum areas. The concern with learning is perhaps more important to early years practitioners than to any other educational practitioners. Adults who work in the Foundation Stage are concerned with creating a bridge between the way children have learned at home and the way they will learn in the more formal and densely populated nursery and reception classes. They want to continue, as far as possible, the beneficial practices of the child's first educators, which have resulted in successful and rapid learning and confident learners. Play as a means of learning is most apparent in the Foundation Stage although it is also seen in Key Stage 1 and sometimes Key Stage 2 classes. The integrated curriculum, the awareness of children as learners and the centrality of play mean that nursery and reception classes are organized in ways that are distinct and different to the other key stages.

The curriculum explained

Each of the four curriculum bodies in the UK – the Qualifications and Assessment Authority (QAA) in England, The Curriculum and Assessment Authority for Wales, the Scottish Consultative Council on the Curriculum and the Northern Ireland Council for Curriculum Examinations and Assessment – have produced guidance about the curriculum for children aged between 3 and 5. There are minor differences between the practices and outcomes that are emphasized but for the most part the sort of curriculum that is advocated in each country is very similar. Although most of the references in this book will be to the English guidelines, readers across the UK and in other countries too should be able to relate the ideas to their particular situation.

Integrating learning

In May 2000 the *Curriculum Guidance for the Foundation Stage* (QCA, 2000b) was published. This sets out what children aged 3 to 5 are expected to learn in nursery settings and reception classes in England. The guidance covers six areas of learning: personal, social and emotional development; communication, language and literacy; mathematical development; knowledge and understanding of the world; physical development; and creative development. This book is concerned with the second area, that of learning, communication, language and literacy. However one of the characteristics of learning is that it often ranges across and goes beyond individual subject areas. For example, learning about numbers will involve being able to use number names and may take place through joining in with number stories, rhymes and songs as well as discrete mathematical activities. So, although children's increasing understanding of number is an aspect of mathematical development, their learning will be supported by experiences in language, literacy and music as well as other areas of the curriculum. These cross-curricular links are an important facet of the curriculum in the Foundation Stage. Although the subject of this book is communication, language and literacy, in keeping with early years practice, links with other areas of learning will be explored.

The statutory curriculum

The curriculum guidance for communication, language and literacy covers the education of children from 3 to 5. It is intended to cover a two-year period, the year that 3- and 4-year-olds spend in nursery settings and the year that 4- and 5-year-olds spend in reception classes. The guidance is arranged as a series of learning objectives ordered by difficulty. There are four levels of difficulty, three of which are known as stepping stones. The final level contains the Early Learning Goals. The four levels are not age specific, but the first two sets of objectives are likely to be covered in the nursery and the final set of stepping stones and the Early Learning Goals will shape the curriculum in the reception class. Not all children spend time in a nursery or other pre-school setting and so, for some children, their first encounter with a planned curriculum will be in the reception class where their learning objectives will be taken from level 3 of the stepping stones, although objectives from the earlier levels may also be applicable. The final level of objectives, the Early Learning Goals for communication language and literacy, lead into the National Curriculum programme of study for English at Key Stage 1 (DfEE/QCA, 1999).

Communication, language and literacy

The curriculum for communication, language and literacy broadly covers learning in and about speaking and listening, reading and writing. However the words *communication* and *language* encompass far more than oral communication or speaking and listening. They serve as a reminder that reading and writing are also communicative and social activities. They suggest that language is a key element of thinking and learning, and that language development should be considered when planning for learning across the curriculum. Therefore, to develop within this area of learning, children will need to learn about speaking and listening, reading and writing as well as learning to read and write and to extend their oral abilities.

Children as learners
Learning at home

By the time children enter the nursery or reception class they have already learned a tremendous amount. They have learned to operate socially within their own immediate and extended families. They have learned about their home and community environment. They know how to communicate with others, ask questions, act on instructions and understand explanations. Most children have experience of stories through encounters with books or via television and videos. They can manipulate physical objects as they play and meet some of their own needs. This list could continue for some time.

Suffice to say, young children have made rapid gains in learning in all the areas of learning that constitute the curriculum for the Foundation Stage, even though they have not followed a planned curriculum.

How children learn

How have they learned so much in such a short space of time? They have learned from the adults around them, their environment and their experiences. Adults have provided them with models of behaviour that can be imitated, explanations of events and experiences and answers to questions. Family members and friends have treated the child as a cognitive being who can, will and wants to learn about the world and how to operate within it, and through their actions and interactions they have shared their own knowledge in ways that are appropriate to a young child's developing understanding. Many of the adults' interactions will have arisen from the child's curiosity about the world and their desire to learn about it. However, young children do not learn only from others. They will have learned by listening, looking, touching and engaging in playful activities with toys and objects. Their learning will have come from a number of sources. They will have developed knowledge, skills and understanding through a variety of learning strategies.

Much of a young child's learning will have taken place in an immediate context. Questions will have arisen from what is seen or touched. Explanations will have been given in relation to what the child is doing or using. As Piaget, Vygotsky and Bruner all agree, young children learn in practical, concrete ways and their learning is located in directly purposeful and relevant situations (Wood, 1988). Abstract learning that is not directly related to the child's own purposes or the immediate and tangible environment, generally occurs after the age of 3 and children need to be led gradually into this next stage of learning. This is when the skills and understanding of those who work in the Foundation Stage are crucial as they begin to lead children away from the familiar and help them to explore the unknown.

Young children are active learners. They interact physically with the world that they live in and play their part in initiating teaching sequences as they try to do something or ask questions. They construct their understanding by taking in information and relating it to what they already know. Learning, particularly young children's learning, is usually mediated through social encounters and interactions. It is a social activity. In addition, what and how children learn is situated in a particular social or cultural context. Different communities and families within that community will emphasize different things. For example, in some homes politeness and good manners may be very important. If this is the case, it is likely that children will learn to be courteous.

The combination of these ideas, that children actively construct understandings and that learning takes place in social settings, has led to a view of learning that is known as social constuctivism (Hiebert and Raphael, 1998). The features of social constructivism are helpful when thinking about the organization of an early years setting and when planning the curriculum. Children will need access to, and opportunities to develop or construct, their learning by engaging in new experiences and then relating this new awareness to what they already know. To do this they will need opportunities to predict outcomes based on their existing knowledge, to evaluate new experiences and to compare new and old information. They will need to be able to ask questions and to follow avenues of enquiry that interest them. They will need opportunities to engage in meaningful exchanges with adults and other children as well as opportunities to see others demonstrate or use skills. They will also need opportunities to appreciate what their teachers value and to understand why those behaviours or practices are important.

Dispositions and attitudes

Thinking about learning is not just about understanding how learning takes place but is also concerned with what should be learned. Children learn skills and knowledge but they also develop feelings and attitudes to what they learn. Katz has called these attitudes 'dispositions' (Katz and Chard, 1989). It is important that children are disposed to be curious, to explore and to enjoy their learning. These dispositions are present in young children when they first enter Foundation Stage settings but they may be damaged if the learning experiences that are provided for them are too easy, too difficult, dull or repetitive. Inappropriate activities may teach children that they are unsuccessful as learners or that learning at school is boring. Positive dispositions grow from experiences that children enjoy and are interested in. They also allow children to be in control and to experience success. In a review of the research about successful learners, Desforges and Abouchaar (2003) found that children who believe in their own ability to learn and whose parents have high aspirations for them are the children most likely to succeed at school. If practitioners can help children to feel confident and have high expectations for the children they work with this will have a significant effect on children's achievement.

Using our understanding of learning to inform teaching

When adults understand how children learn before they embark on planned learning in the more formal setting of a nursery or reception class, they can appreciate the learning strategies that children already have. They can then incorporate these strategies into the learning opportunities they provide and the teaching methods they employ. The following lists suggest some principles which practitioners use to inform their planning for communication, language and literacy.

Young children:

- learn actively through looking, listening and doing;
- are motivated to learn;
- are curious and willing to explore the unfamiliar;
- learn through taking risks;
- learn through practice;
- can attend with intensity for considerable periods when they are interested;
- learn in collaboration with others;
- learn through asking questions;
- can take the initiative in learning;
- learn things that are relevant and enjoyable to them;
- remember things that are important to them;
- learn about the things that are prioritized by those around them;
- learn when they feel secure and confident;
- learn in different ways; and
- learn at different rates.

The adults who enable children to learn in informal situations at home:

- give children time;
- provide experiences and materials that stimulate children;
- provide children with models of how to do things;
- provide opportunities for children to practise and apply their skills;
- respect and attend to children's questions;
- provide answers to questions;
- provide explanations about social practices and activities;
- expect children to learn and acknowledge their learning;
- provide an environment in which it is safe to take risks; and
- respond and provide for children in ways that are appropriate to the child's understanding and interests.

Play

Play as a context for learning

Play can provide children with valuable learning experiences. Although children can and do learn in other ways, play is an established and accepted part of the early years curriculum. It has become such a key part of provision in the Foundation Stage because it is pleasurable and practical, and so is attractive to young children. It gives children the opportunity to take control as they engage with activities and materials, and to decide how the resources will be used. They can express and explore their own ideas without pressure or censure. In play, adults are usually participants rather than being in charge of the activity or the outcome. Play is voluntary and in play situations children are able to take risks. During play there are no judgements about right or wrong answers or ways of doing things. Play provides a context within which children can construct meanings and understandings and develop positive attitudes to school and learning.

Play and work

Not all play situations give rise to play. If children do not know what to do with the materials, if they find the materials or the activity dull or unappealing, or if the adult controls the situation leaving no scope for personal interpretation or creativity, play will not take place, or at least it will not be regarded as play by the participant. Play is as much an attitude of mind as it is an activity. Reading books can be an enjoyable activity that is undertaken voluntarily. Readers are personally involved, they interpret what they read in ways that link to their own experience and understanding. Yet reading is often thought of as work in school. Think of the delight that young children have in their nightly bedtime story and how some children choose to pour over a picture book long before they can read. Amongst our friends we probably all know someone who enjoys solving mathematical problems like those to be found in the weekend newspapers or tackling crosswords or other word games in their leisure time. Indeed, there are magazines dedicated to word and other puzzles. Yet letters, words and numbers in school may be considered dull and hard. Perhaps we need to examine the distinction that is often made between work and play. It might not be as straightforward as it seems. Work can be play if the conditions for play are met and the participant approaches the activity with eagerness and with an expectation of enjoyment. In addition to thinking of ways in which play can be used to foster learning, perhaps we could also give more time to considering how to present learning as an engaging and enjoyable pursuit, and how to reflect the qualities of play in learning experiences.

Structured and unstructured play

Some purists might take exception to this blurred distinction between play and work believing that play should have no real purpose or goal and that children's play should be completely free from adult involvement. This point of view has led practitioners to question the play provision that they make for young children. They are sometimes anxious about structuring children's play by planning for it in ways that will develop children's learning. They worry that by interfering in children's play they will be devaluing play and transforming play into work. This is not a very productive debate, particularly if one accepts that work and play can overlap and if one acknowledges that all play is structured by the materials that are available to the participants. For example, the sort of clothes that are available for dressing up, whether in school or at home, will shape children's role play and exploration of other identities. When children put on yellow hard hats they likely to become builders, firefighters or miners but are unlikely to consider themselves doctors or shopkeepers. We know, from children's productive learning experiences out of school and from the research, that young children learn well when they are actively interacting with others (Wood and Bennett, 1999). Without planning, careful selection of the number and type of resources and without adult interaction it would be very difficult to provide challenging, fresh and stimulating play opportunities for a class of 20–30 young children.

Accepting that all play is structured has implications for practitioners. It means that they need to take care when they make choices about the play opportunities they provide and how these are to be resourced. They need to provide resources that will appeal to children and to ensure that resources are changed regularly in order to provide children with a variety of play opportunities. The choices that they make will affect what children learn, so practitioners need to be aware of how the resources will support the children's play and guide their learning. Then these likely outcomes need to be matched to what would benefit the children.

Free and directed play

Rather than thinking about structured and unstructured play it is perhaps more productive to think about free and directed play. Free play is 'the opportunity to explore and investigate materials and situations for oneself' (Moyles, 1989: 14). Directed play is led by an adult who shows children how to do something or joins in their play to guide it or move it on. The adult might take the lead in the children's role play in the vet's surgery. She might take on the role of the veterinary nurse engaging pet owners in conversation, making notes about pets' ailments and assisting the vet. She will be doing this with the intention of giving the children a model of behaviour that they can incorporate into their subsequent free or undirected play in the vet's surgery. Such interventions prevent the children's play becoming repetitive and stimulate the children to extend their understanding.

Productive play opportunities are usefully planned as a sequence containing both free and directed activities. The children's first encounter with a new set of materials or a new resource might be free. This allows the children to explore the properties of the materials or the possibilities of the situation. The second encounter might be supported or led by an adult in order to channel the children's behaviour. The next time the children access the same play activity they can try out this new idea for themselves and so extend their understanding. Moyles (1989) suggests that this balance of free and directed play can continue for some time, giving children opportunities to restructure their present level of understanding at each stage as they receive and experiment with new ideas.

Types of play

There are a number of different types of play. Piaget (1951) distinguished between practice play, symbolic play and play with rules, and a further category, constructive play, was added by Smilansky (1968). Practice play includes such things as repeatedly rebuilding construction toys in the same way, repeating rhymes or the repetition of the same marks on a page when experimenting with writing. Symbolic play involves creating or using objects to represent ideas, situations or other objects. For example, a block could be used to represent a car or a child could pretend to be a superhero. Pretend, fantasy and socio-dramatic (role play involving two or more children) play are all forms of symbolic play. In constructive play objects are manipulated to create something new. A collage can be made from scrap or waste paper, cloth and other material, or homes may be built out of cardboard boxes or wooden bricks. The children themselves may decide the rules for play or they use or adapt rules from traditional games such as hopscotch or bingo.

Each of these different types of play can extend development and skills in the social, intellectual, creative and physical domains. They also have a part to play in communication, language and literacy. Socio-dramatic play involves communicating with one or more play partners and using language to present an acquired identity. Through taking on a role, children may begin to develop empathy. Such play may also develop children's story-telling and story-making skills as they develop a narrative, located in a particular setting and involving a sequence of actions and events. Constructive play may, although it does not need to, involve cooperating and interacting with others. It develops motor skills and coordination. It can also be used to represent ideas and as a response to stories. Because children have the freedom to enter unfamiliar worlds and explore new ideas through their play, it might also be a means of enhancing their creativity and imagination. These are essential if children are to read with understanding and write with flair. Play with rules may encourage interaction and if the children set the rules of the play for themselves they may be developing skills of negotiation, appreciating alternative points of view and planning.

Planning for play

Educators have a critical role in creating opportunities for learning through play. They need to provide play situations and to consider how they will support children as they engage with the resources they have provided. Practitioners need a high level of pedagogical understanding in order to create a challenging curriculum and respond to and develop children's learning.

The sort of play activities that are provided need to be carefully planned. Each one will need a clear purpose or expected learning outcome. When selecting activities practitioners need to think about the way each activity will help to extend children's experiences and learning. Do they build on previous activities? Do they have the scope to be altered so that there can be progression of learning during the life of the activity? At the planning stage it is also important to think about how the children's learning will be assessed, what will be assessed and who will undertake the assessments. It might also be possible to involve the children in making decisions about the choice of play areas. Certainly, thought will be given to the interests of the class and making play relevant to these particular children in this particular locality. The resources that are selected will need to support the intended learning, be enticing to the children and reflect the cultural and language diversity of the children in the class and the wider community. The activities and the resources will need to appeal to and be appropriate to boys, girls and children with special educational needs. When planning it is important to think about how far the resources will support children's independent play and learning. Will the children need support and, if so, how will this be provided? If adults will need to participate in the activity or support some children by sensitively timed interventions, this too will need to be considered at the planning stage.

Valuing play

Children need time to explore and engage with carefully planned play activities, particularly if one plans for a cycle of free and directed encounters as suggested by Moyles (1989). It is often easier to allow for lengthy blocks of time in nursery settings, but it can be more difficult in some reception classes where there is sometimes greater emphasis on more formal learning or where blocks of time are allocated to specific curriculum areas. Children's play can be interrupted by adult-directed sessions or routines. Sometimes routines can be flexible. For example drinks and biscuits can be accessed by the children when they are thirsty rather than being timetabled to occur at a particular time. Similarly, outdoor activities can be available for most of the day rather than being timetabled for all the class at the same time. As well as giving children time to concentrate and engage in periods of sustained play, more flexible arrangements give children the opportunity to make choices.

When play is frequently interrupted by adult-led activities, which often focus on literacy and numeracy, children may be learning that more formal activities or *work* is more important than play. This can be reinforced if adults are more frequently to be found seated at or guiding activities that are more obviously linked to literacy and numeracy. Towards the end of the Foundation Stage or in some reception classes, play may be allocated to the afternoon or a short time at the end of each day. Sometimes children are allowed to *play* after they have finished their *work*. This undermines the status of play in children's minds and reflects a true lack of understanding or confidence in the value and centrality of play to learning. When play is planned for in this way, both work and play can suffer. Children can rush through their work in order to play and, because they can see that play is not valued or that it is regarded as easy, they may not give their play serious attention and so fail to derive its full potential as a means of learning.

Adult roles

Once play activities have been set up, adults have a key role in making sure that children gain the full benefit from them. They can support children's learning in a number of ways. It is important that their involvement focuses on supporting and extending learning through play rather than interrupting it. If adults join in without being tuned in to what the children are doing they can sometimes ask well-meaning but intrusive questions that focus on teaching, testing learning or that miss the point of what the children have been doing. For example, imagine that a child shows the adult a menu that he has written in the role-play area. If the adult responds by saying, 'That's very good' or 'Look at the beautiful C that you have made. Can you see any other Cs in the room?', a valuable opportunity to engage in a dialogue with the child, to listen to what he wants to say about his writing or to participate in and sustain his role play might have been lost. It is likely that interventions that are sympathetic to the children's endeavours and appropriate to their needs will have been preceded by a period of observation during which the practitioner can focus on the children, the strategies they are using as well as the learning that can be seen.

Involvement in play can take many forms from indirect to direct. The least intrusive of these is acting as an onlooker (Roskos and Neuman, 1993). Here the adult remains outside the children's play but offers acknowledgement or encouragement through brief verbal comments or non-verbal gestures. This may encourage children to sustain their concentration. Another indirect role is to facilitate further learning by changing the resources or suggesting new directions for the play. If children are left to play on their own without adults' observing them and assessing the quality of their experience, the children may repeat the same forms of play. Effective intervention through the introduction of new resources or the introduction of a new dilemma or challenge which channels the children's play in productive directions can motivate children and extend their learning. In order to help children remain in role or to encourage fuller participation, adults might model appropriate behaviour in role-play situations. This can be done by, for example, writing down a telephone message or reading a story to one of the dolls. This modelling can be carried out without fully participating in the children's play but it is likely that after seeing this model the children will imitate it. Sometimes the adult will intervene in order to monitor the way in which children are negotiating their ideas or formulating rules. This form of intervention will enable the adult to support individuals as well as groups. It will depend on the adult being available and keeping a check on activities to see if mediation or assistance are needed.

Full participation in play alongside the children is rarer than other forms of intervention but it is a powerful way of fostering learning. The adult can follow the children's lead and fit in with the direction their play is taking while also suggesting extensions and adding props. They can act as a catalyst and initiate new ideas, but in ways that fit in with the children's thinking. When adults join in with activities they can discuss ideas, model practices and behaviour, and introduce new vocabulary. Playing alongside children legitimizes play and encourages children to see play as something that is valued. It avoids the work–play divide that can arise when adult participation focuses more on formal *work* activities. The most directive end of the intervention continuum is when adults act as play leaders (Roskos and Neuman, 1993). They plan ahead with the intention of introducing specific props, demonstrations and explicit directions.

Knowing what to plan for and knowing when and how to intervene depends on knowing the children and being aware of the processes and strategies that they use during their play. This information is gained through observing children as they play. Observation also enables adults to evaluate the success of the planned activities, to assess children's needs and to plan for progression of learning and the development of the activity.

Play is a valuable means of learning in early years classrooms. It offers opportunities for children to develop their learning in enjoyable ways. If the potential of play as a means of learning is to be realized, it needs to be carefully planned and supported by sensitive and well-timed adult interventions. The nature of play means that it fits easily into the socio-constructivist view of learning and encourages the development of positive dispositions such as curiosity, perseverance and imagination that are excellent strategies for learning.

Organizing for learning in nursery and pre-school settings

Types of pre-school provision

Provision in the Foundation Stage covers nursery settings and reception classes. In some schools nursery and reception have been combined to form early years units. However, in many cases reception classes and other forms of pre-school provision are separate. The organization and staffing of nursery and other pre-school settings is often significantly different to that of reception classes. This makes a difference to the curriculum that is offered and the way that it is taught. There are many types of pre-school provision available for children to attend between the ages of 3 and 5. These include:

- nursery classes in state schools;
- reception classes in state schools;
- state nursery schools;
- childminders;

- pre-schools;
- playgroups;
- private nursery schools;
- day care centres; and
- workplace nurseries.

Children may attend part time or full time and some children, particularly those who go to day centres, may spend an extended day there. This often matches the working hours of their parents. Whatever the setting, if it receives nursery education grant funding it is required to offer provision that enables children to progress through the stepping stones towards the Early Learning Goals (QCA, 2000b).

Layout and resources

Different forms of provision will have different levels of resources and facilities available. Some pre-schools may have limited space and resources because they do not receive the same level of funding as nursery schools and they may not be the sole users of the building in which they are based. The particular philosophy of some nursery practitioners may influence the way that space is used. For example, in Montessori nurseries there is probably less emphasis on developing children's relationships with each other and on group work than in local education authority (LEA) nurseries. This is because Montessori thought that working alone helped children to become independent learners. She considered that when children were completely absorbed in what they were doing this was learning at its best. Montessori nurseries also have specialized equipment and resources designed by and advocated by their founder. In Steiner schools there is a strong emphasis on natural materials. The amount of commercial equipment is minimal and outdoors children will have logs and tree trunks for climbing and balancing. Story-telling rather than story-reading is an important part of the Steiner curriculum, and this impacts on the activities that are offered and the resources that are used.

In most pre-school settings the room or rooms that are used are divided into areas. A large open space in which children can gather together as a class or in a large group is important for listening to stories, listening and speaking, shared reading and shared writing. There will normally be a reading and library area, a mark-making or writing area, an imaginative play area, a construction area, an art or creative area, a sensory area, and sand and water containers. Information and communications technologies (ICT) equipment, including computers and tape recorders, will be placed around the room and may be found in the reading, writing and role-play areas. Some nurseries may have large indoor equipment such as benches or a ball pool for physical activities. Many nurseries have such equipment plus wheeled toys in the outdoor area. The outdoor area is an outdoor classroom and so should provide opportunities for learning that mirror those provided indoors. Outdoors there can be a sandpit and a water trough, a wildlife area, and covered areas for reading, drawing, painting and construction. The outdoor area can be used as much as indoors when it is planned for and resourced well, even in poorer weather. There is a Danish saying which reminds us that 'it's not the weather that's the problem, it's the clothes we wear'! Both indoors and outdoors there will be tables and chairs where children can work on group and independent activities using a variety of resources.

Organization of the day

In most nursery settings a typical session lasts for two and a half hours and most children attend for one session each day. At the start of the session children will come into a room where activities have already been set up. They may select one of these and it is usually possible for the adult who has brought them to join in with them for a short time if they wish. At some point during the session all the children will gather together for a shared activity such a story or rhymes or music. This may also be a time when new or unfamiliar activities are pointed out to the children. The children may then return to their activities. The outdoor area is usually opened once all the children have arrived and is available until about half an hour before the session ends. The last half an hour of the session is spent on tidying things away and coming together as a whole group or in smaller adult-led groups to engage in a quiet, reflective activity. There are variations in this pattern and nurseries devise a framework that suits the number and availability of staff and the resources that are available. In some nurseries, particularly those following the high scope principles, at the start of the session children plan their time by selecting more than one activity from those available and recording their choices on a noticeboard. They will then do their first activity. At the end of the session there will be an opportunity to talk about what they have done during the session and reflect on their experiences and their learning.

Organizing for learning in the reception class

The statutory age for starting school is at the beginning of the term after the child's fifth birthday, so some children with summer birthdays could begin school in Year 1 and if their parents wished miss out on the Foundation Stage altogether. Most children do spend time in reception classes, and many and increasing numbers of children spend time in one or more pre-school settings. Figure 1.1 shows the differences in provision found in nursery and reception classes.

	Nursery	Reception
Attendance	Mostly part time	Full time after the first few weeks
Number of hours spent at the setting each day	2 hours 30 minutes	6 hours
Number of adults	1 teacher + 1 full-time nursery assistant to 26 children	1 teacher + 1 part-time teaching assistant to 30 children
Curriculum planning	Often linked to areas/resources Follows the *Curriculum Guidance for the Foundation Stage*	Beginning to become subject focused Follows the *Curriculum Guidance for the Foundation Stage* The literacy hour and numeracy sessions are in place in the summer term
Layout	Children do not have allocated seats Outdoors and indoors used daily	Every child has a seat at a table Most equipment is indoors
Resources	Large equipment available most of the time	Large equipment available some of the time
Grouping	Small groups, individual work, a small amount of whole class	About 50% of the time in small groups and individual activities and 50% of the time as a whole class
Types of groups	Generally flexible, selected by the adults, friendship groups, child initiated	Some flexibility but children may be in fairly fixed ability groups for CLL
Pupil autonomy	Most children choose most of the activities themselves There is a large range of activities to choose from	The children are likely to be directed to activities The number of activities offered at any one time will be limited and probably no more than 5

Figure 1.1 *The differences in provision in nursery and reception classes*

The amount of time, the type of equipment and the adult support available varies considerably between settings, but they are all expected to help children develop their knowledge and understanding of communication, language and literacy. One of the key differences between reception classes and other forms of pre-school provision is that during the reception year children are prepared for and then allocated a dedicated hour each day for literacy. This does not have to result in formal ways of teaching children. Practitioners have resisted the pressure, sometimes exerted on them in the early days of the National Literacy Strategy, to relinquish a practical and play-based curriculum in favour of one that prioritizes pencil-and-paper tasks. The value of the Foundation Stage approach has been recognized and in a recent report (Sanders et al., 2005) the authors recommended that some of the practices should be extended into Year 1.

> The amount of time children in Year 1 spend sitting still and listening to the teacher should be reduced. Year 1 teachers should be encouraged to increase opportunities for active, independent learning and learning through play.
>
> Schools should encourage staff to adopt similar routines, expectations and activities in Reception and Year 1. School managers should allocate resources to enable children in Year 1 to experience some play-based activities that give access to opportunities such as sand and water, role play, construction and outdoor learning. (Sanders et al., 2005: 9.5)

Conclusion

In this chapter I have attempted to describe the curriculum, teaching style and organization that can be found in the many settings that provide for children in the Foundation Stage. This provides the context for the activities and suggestions about developing communication, language and literacy that are outlined in the remaining chapters of the book.

Further reading

Anning, A. and Edwards, A. (2006) *Promoting Children's Learning from Birth to Five: Developing the New Early Years Professional.* 2nd edn. Maidenhead: Open University Press.
In this book the authors focus on literacy and mathematical development to illustrate ways of working with young children.

Bruce, T. (ed.) (2006) *Early Childhood – A Guide for Students*. London: Sage.
  This book was written for students on early childhood courses and is an
    ideal introductory text.

Edgington, M. (2004) *The Foundation Stage Teacher in Action: Teaching 3, 4 and 5
  Year Olds*. 3rd edn. London: Paul Chapman Publishing.
This is an up-to-date and practical examination of the role of practitioners in
  the Foundation Stage.

Smidt, S. (2002) *A Guide to Early Years Practice*. 2nd edn. Abingdon: Routledge/
  Falmer.
This is a practical and accessible guide to learning and teaching in the
  Foundation Stage.

Chapter 2

Speaking and listening

Introduction

This chapter examines the development of speaking and listening from birth to 5. In it I look at how talk is used to engage with others and to learn. The chapter describes how practitioners can contribute to children's language development. There are a number of suggestions for activities for developing oral language in nursery settings and reception classes.

Language

What is language and what are its characteristics? At the simplest level there are two important aspects of language: the structural elements and its uses. The structural elements are sounds, words and a system of rules that govern the way the language works. The rules or grammar of a language govern such things as word structure, for example, when to use *walk* rather than *walked*, word choice, for example, when to use *which* rather than *that,* and word order. Being able to use the grammar of a language enables speakers to combine words to produce meaningful utterances or oral texts that may contain a few words or thousands of sentences.

Being able to understand and produce language or to listen and speak enables us to interact socially with others. It enables us to communicate with others by conveying and receiving meanings. Perhaps most importantly, it enables us to learn by exploring, narrating and reflecting on experiences and knowledge with others and with ourselves.

Language acquisition

The acquisition of a first language is probably the most complex skill anyone ever learns. The speed and apparent ease with which most children learn to listen and speak can fool us into underestimating how much they accomplish in a very short space of time.

By the time children enter the Foundation Stage they will have already acquired a substantial vocabulary and most of the grammatical structures of their native language. They will also have used oral language to interact with others, to exchange meanings and to begin to make sense of the world in which they are growing up. Regardless of their social background, children will have enjoyed and benefited from rich linguistic experiences that enable them to use language in a range of ways in a variety of circumstances (Tizard and Hughes, 2002).

Emergent language

There are variations in the rates at which children develop and go through the stages of language development but, even if the age at which children acquire vocabulary and aspects of grammar varies slightly, the stages are always the same. Whatever the precise age at which different elements of language are manifested it is true that between the ages of 0 and 5 years children's language development is rapid. The productive use of language gains in momentum after the age of about 12 months but even before this children have been actively learning about the language community they have entered.

At about 2 months babies begin to make cooing noises which sound like long sequences of vowel sounds preceded by a consonant-like sound. At about 3 months these are replaced by sounds that are much more definite and controlled. Babies seem to take pleasure in experimenting with these noises. From about 6 months onwards, children begin to produce repetitive sequences of syllables such as *babababa* and later combinations of syllables as in *bama*. Some of the syllable combinations that are produced sound similar to adult words, especially *mama* and *dada* which adults usually interpret as *mummy* and *daddy*. Cooing, vocal play and babbling precede words although babbling may continue for a short time after the production of the first word.

In the first 12 months and before children articulate their first word they have been learning about other features of adult language. There is evidence to show that at the age of 6 months children are picking up features of the melody and rhythm of the adult language and that by 9 months strings of syllables are being pronounced in conversation-like ways (Crystal, 1997).

Even before this, from about 2 months onwards, children begin to show signs of understanding the tone of voice that adults use when they are angry or when they are pleased, and they show some recognition of the names of family members.

Vocabulary

Between 10 and 15 months most children produce their first understandable words. These often contain repeated syllables as in *mama* and *papa* or they may consist of single syllables that resemble words such as *da* for dog or *ba* for baby. The majority of the child's first 50 words are words that can be used to name important objects or events, with a much smaller percentage being used to describe actions such as *gone* or *eat*. Other early words are those that help the child achieve personal desires like *more* or *up* or that are used as part of a communicative interaction such as *ta* or *bye-bye*. During the acquisition of the first 50 words and subsequently, children understand many more words than they can produce and their comprehension continues to grow rapidly. At 18 months the number of words that are understood outnumber the words that are produced by about 5 to 1 but by the age of 3 years the ratio narrows to about 1.5 to 1 (Crystal, 1997).

Over the next four years and throughout their lives children continue to add to their productive vocabulary. At about 18 months children may be able to use 50 words, by 19 months this is likely to have increased to 100, growing to 200 by the age of 21 months and 300 at age 3. During the third year children's active vocabulary grows to a remarkable 3,000 words and at the age of 5 children can use about 5,000 words, although this figure varies between researchers as so many words become very difficult to count. This is indeed an achievement and shows that young children are well on their way to reaching the normal adult active vocabulary of about 50,000 words.

Grammar

From the time that children produce their first words, speaking plays an increasingly important role in communications between children and caregivers. Initially, children produce single-word utterances as they initiate and respond to conversations, but by about 18 months they are producing two-word utterances. These observe grammatical conventions for ordering words in sentences. For example, children might say *dog eat*, meaning *the dog is eating*, which follows the subject verb construction. Not observing this rule and instead producing *eat dog* could result in a very different interpretation. At this stage children begin to incorporate prepositions into their speech particularly, *in* and *on*. Two-word utterances are followed by three- and four-word sentences which are more elaborate and allow meanings to be expressed more clearly.

Between 3 and 4 years children learn more and more about grammar. They begin to produce increasingly longer and more complex sentences. They begin to link clauses using conjunctions such as *and, so, then, when, if* and *before*. They can formulate questions. They include articles in their speech. They use negative constructions such as *won't* and *can't* and draw upon auxiliary verbs such as *will, can* and *shall* in their utterances. They begin to use comparatives such as *biggest* and *smaller*. They also begin to use a simple future tense which often initially appears as *I'm gonna*. Hypothetical future constructions such as *If it rains we can watch a video* appear later at about age 4. Around this time mistakes such as *goed* and *foots* begin to disappear as children acquire irregular forms of verbs and nouns. However some over-regularization may persist for a number of years and it is not uncommon for 8-year-olds to say *I falled over*. Between 4 and 5 years of age children use an increasing number of pronouns and begin to sort out their correct use, eliminating mistakes such as *Me tired*. After the age of 5 children begin to learn about, and use, the passive form and can say and understand sentences such as *I got smacked* but mastery of the passive takes some time and children may still find this difficult at age 9.

Using language

There is more to language development than vocabulary-building or acquiring a knowledge of grammar, although these are important. Their significance lies in the way in which a widening vocabulary and access to increasingly complex grammatical forms enables children to use oral language for an increasing number of purposes, with a growing realization of how to use language in different situations.

Children's first words are used to label people, objects or events. They show children recognizing and making sense of their experiences and environment, and communicating this to others. They enable children to develop conversational behaviour as others usually respond to their utterances. However, these early words are related to the context in which they occur and they are not usually part of a sustained dialogue. They are imprecise and the hearer often has to interpret them. *Boo* may mean *book*. It might also be a signal for a game. Although children's utterances remain largely context dependent until about the age of 2, their two-, three- and four-word utterances and use of prepositions allows children to begin to communicate their thoughts and feelings as in *cold*, *want hat, want hat on*. As their vocabulary increases, children's speech becomes less dependent on the context and children are able to convey ideas and recall or narrate their experiences as in *nana say silly doggy!*, a recollection of hearing granny talking to the family pet.

From the age of 3 onwards children's learning about, and use of, language enables them to add subtlety and complexity to their utterances, through the increasingly intricate use of tense, plurals, conjunctions, auxiliary verbs and conjunctions. By this stage they can initiate, maintain and join in conversations of some sophistication. They use questions to ask for help and information. They are using language to learn. The acquisition of words such as *because*, *so* and *then* allows children to use language to explain, *that why Tessa comed*, and to argue. From about 4 years of age children are able to use language independent of context. Their ability to use conjunctions and comparatives to express relationships and use hypothetical future constructions enables children to use language to persuade, reason, hypothesize and speculate, all of which show that children are using language to think. Also at this stage, children become increasingly adept at adapting their language to suit their audience and the situation. Children use language very differently when playing with friends, talking to a parent, talking to a baby and talking to a teacher. Charting children's language acquisition enables us to see how the structural gains that children make allow them to use language for a greater variety of purposes. This is summarized in Figure 2.1. There are connections between the greater use that children are able to make of their oral language skills and the curriculum for communication, language and literacy for pupils in the Foundation Stage where practitioners are expected to make provision for children to use language to communicate and to learn.

Activity

Can you remember how you learned to talk? Do you know when you began to talk and what your first words were? What contribution did members of your family make to your language development? Did they influence your interest in language?

Language for thinking and learning

It is easy to see the communicative and social purposes for language. In the early stages of language development we can see children using language to:

■ get others to attend to their needs;

- control the behaviour of others; and
- establish and maintain relationships through language interactions.

Understanding how language is used for thinking is less obvious. Of course language is used to express ideas and learning, but how does it foster thought?

As the size of children's vocabulary grows and they gain control of an increasing range of grammatical structures, they are able to use language to talk about events beyond their immediate experience. They are able to describe events that are remembered, predicted or conjured up from their imaginations. When they can use language in this way, language becomes a symbol system in which words can stand for objects and people even when they are not present. It allows them to revisit and explore events and ideas, and express and refine their thoughts about them. Language as a symbol system also enables children to name and talk about emotions and experiences such as fairness, disappointment and honesty that cannot easily be represented in other ways. Bruner (1986) suggested that adults encourage children to use language for thinking and provide them with a model for doing so through their interactions. When adults talk to children they use language to help them make sense of situations, reflect on what they know and help them to deepen their understanding of events and experiences. Their comments help children to clarify and manipulate their experiences and ideas as well as showing them how to organize, generalize and categorize. Talking with others allows for the oral exploration of ideas. When they talk, participants may change or refine their views as they explain and justify what they think and listen to others' opinions and comments. This is an important way of developing one's own learning and understanding.

Bruner (1986) suggested that as children use language to communicate, they are also coming to understand how language works. They develop metalinguistic awareness which enables them to think about language and its conventions. Even babies at the stages of cooing and babbling are exploring conversational behaviour. Later, children begin to think more about what they say. For example, by the age of 4 most children begin to play with language by inventing words and making and appreciating jokes. From about the age of 3 onwards children begin to recognize that there may be a difference in what the listener knows and what the speaker knows, and so there are occasions when it is necessary to be more explicit. This developing understanding of audience provides further evidence of children reflecting on their own use of language.

Vygotsky (1986), who also regarded language as essential to thinking and learning, suggested that, although language and thought are originally sep-

Age in months	Vocabulary	Grammar	Scope
2–12	Cooing, vocal play, babbling		understand the meaning of utterances made by others aware of how to hold a conversation
10–15	First words	Largely names or nouns	context dependent language for communication
18–24		Combining words Showing awareness of word order Beginning to learn prepositions such as *in* and *on*	context dependent language for communication able to communicate thoughts and feelings
24–36		Three- and four-word sentences	Less context dependent expressing ideas narrating
30–36		Word endings	
36–48	Continuing to add to vocabulary	More complex sentences Questions Auxiliary verbs Negative constructions Articles Expressing relationships through use of conjunctions to join sentences Use of comparatives Simple future tense	less context dependent language for learning asking for help and information explaining arguing
48–60		Irregularities such as *he goed* start to disappear Hypothetical future constructions Irregular verbs	Able to use language independently from its context Language for thinking Aware of audience Vary language according to situation Able to persuade, reason, speculate, negotiate
60+		Passives begin to develop	

Figure 2.1 *The aspects of language acquired by the time children are 5 years old*

arate, they are interrelated and that language very quickly becomes a tool for thought. He asked, is it possible to think without language and is it possible to speak without thinking? He proposed that when children go through the stage of talking aloud to themselves to explain and describe what they are doing and seeing, from about the age of 12 months, they are trying to control, plan, recall and predict. They are classifying and ordering their feelings and experiences. As children get older these monologues become more abbreviated and gradually become internalized. Their need to talk through their actions and experiences is gradually replaced by thinking things through but language still plays a part in this thinking. 'Speech in infancy is the direct antecedent of thinking at a later stage' (Vygotsky, 1986: 21).

To appreciate the connection between thought and language it can help to consider that we all use internal language when we need to:

- think through different ideas;
- organize our thoughts;
- tell ourselves what to do; and
- think about our feelings.

This internal, cognitive use of language is about exploring and combining ideas. It is often tentative and the outcome may be be uncertain and open to change. The contradictions or errors in one's thinking may become apparent as one articulates possible conclusions. This may lead to further thought and exploration of ideas. Curiosity, and the willingness to reflect and to investigate are vital for learning, and those who work with young children are keen to foster these dispositions and habits. They can do this by encouraging children to use talk to think by inviting children to engage in different mental activities as they play and work. They can talk to children about their activities and may ask questions, but these are open questions to which there are not necessarily any right answers. The important thing is that these are collaborative discussions during which children develop their understanding. Below are a list of types of talk which are allied to thinking and some open questions which adults can use to prompt different types of thinking.

- Explain – Why do you think that ... ? Will you show me how to ... ?
- Rethink – Is there another way ... ?
- Recall – Did you notice what happened when ... ?
- Predict – What would happen if ... ?
- Reason – I wonder why that happened? What do you think ... ?
- Evaluate – Which suggestion is best and why ... ?
- Plan – What could you do next time ... ?

These sorts of questions will arise in activities across the curriculum. For example, explanations of one's own ideas or evaluations of the ideas of others may occur in circle time and predictions and reasoning in science activities.

Accent, dialect and standard English

The structural elements of language are sounds, words and grammar. When describing speech we often refer to accent and dialect. Accent refers to the way that words are pronounced. Dialect refers to vocabulary items and grammatical constructions. A person's accent usually provides clues to their geographical origin and social class. You may be familiar with the long *oo* sound that is characteristic of many accents in the north of England which gives rise to words such as *book* pronounced in a way that rhymes with *soup* which contrasts with the shorter *u* sound used in the south of England. There is a neutral accent in English which provides no clues to the speaker's geographical origins. This is known as received pronunciation.

There are many different dialects in English which each contain some distinctive words and use particular grammatical constructions. Words such as *nowt* (nothing), *mardy* (soft) and *youse* (the plural form of you) are found in dialects spoken in the north of England, East Anglia and Northern Ireland respectively. These words will not necessarily be understood by all speakers of English and so are non-standard. Grammatical constructions that occur in different regional dialects are often associated with lack of agreement between the subject and the verb as in, *they was*, the formation of the past tense as in, *I done it* and the way negatives are formed for example the use of, *aint*.

Standard English is a variety or dialect of English that does not reveal the speaker's geographical or social origins because it contains no regional words or constructions. It can be spoken in any accent. It is the variety of English that carries most social prestige. Most speakers use a combination of regional dialect and standard English when they are speaking, although in more formal situations they may deliberately choose standard English words and grammar. Standard English is most often used in written English where spelling and punctuation are also expected to conform to the rules of written English.

Young children may use non-standard grammar when they start nursery or school. They may still be learning about the rules of English. As they explore the rules they often produce words such as *seed* and *goed* instead of *saw* and *went*. Their confusion reflects their awareness that *ed* is often used to mark the past tense but their inexperience with language means that they overuse this rule because they have not yet fully mastered all the irregular forms in English.

Adults who work with young children may have to make decisions about if and how to help children use standard English. In and out of school, children have a great deal of exposure to standard English through story tapes or compact discs (CDs), television and books, and so are familiar with it but may not use it. When they first begin to write they may include non-standard grammatical constructions and community or regional dialect words in their writing. In the early stages of writing they *say* what their writing conveys and so there is a strong relationship between their own speech and writing. As children become more familiar with the conventions of written language through their encounters with written texts and as they hear and see adults modelling writing, they increasingly use standard vocabulary and grammar in their own writing just as they move towards standard spelling and use of punctuation.

> ## Activity
> Are there times when you are particularly conscious of the way in which you use language? Have you ever tried to modify the way you speak? How does your language change in different contexts?

English as an additional language

Acquiring an additional language

More than 100 languages are spoken by citizens and children living in the UK (Crystal, 1997) and so it is likely that many children in nursery and reception classes are learning English as an additional language (EAL). These children will be at different stages of learning English as an additional language. Some children will be bilingual from birth because they have had extensive experience of two or more languages; others will be in the very early stages of acquiring English as an additional language. Children who speak a language other than English at home and have had little sustained contact with English are already aware of the communicative purpose of language and understand that being able to communicate depends on acquiring vocabulary and grammatical structures. This understanding and their familiarity with English from the media and encounters with people in the community help them to understand and use English very rapidly. Although they go through the same stages as children who are acquiring their first language, they do this at an accelerated rate. Cummins (2000) suggested that it takes children between two and four years to become conversationally fluent in an additional language but it may take a further three years to become proficient in the cognitive and academic use of language.

Initially EAL learners go through a silent period. This is a time of active listening during which their capacity to understand what they hear develops. During this period children may say nothing or very little, but as their confidence increases they will begin to communicate through the use of single words such as *yes*, *no* and *me*. Gradually bilingual learners begin to put two and three words together. Initially this word order might temporarily reflect the grammatical patterns of their first language. Just as with first language learning children, they move from two- and three-word utterances to much more extended communications as they include prepositions, pronouns, conjunctions and draw on a growing vocabulary in their speech.

Provision for bilingual learners

Children who are learning an additional language benefit from exposure to language and talk that is understandable because it is linked to objects that are visible and activities that are practical. In early years settings children engage in practical and playful activities alongside other children and adults who talk about the activity and what is happening. Children hear language in context. They also benefit from the routines, ongoing activities and repeated language that are part of the daily life of nursery or reception classes. These provide children with the opportunity to become familiar with often used words and phrases and to understand their meaning. Speaking and listening activities that are provided for all children, such as those suggested towards the end of this chapter, provide opportunities for hearing language in context, hearing models of language provided by children and adults, and hearing words and grammatical structures repeated.

As well as providing opportunities for oral language there are a number of simple things that practitioners can do to support the learning of English as an additional language. These include:

- making use of facial expressions, gesture and eye contact when talking;
- supporting talk and explanations with visual props;
- repeating or rephrasing questions and information;
- having a rich store of tapes of stories and rhymes so that children can listen to and join in with the language of books, poems and songs;
- making use of response partners to provide less threatening talk opportunities;
- allowing thinking time when asking questions;
- using resources that reflect linguistic and cultural variety; and
- creating an environment in which children feel confident enough to have a go with their new language.

It is important that children's first languages are respected and supported at school. Bilingualism is an advantage, not a disadvantage. Cummins (2000: 160) writes that 'bilinguals have advantages in thinking styles, particularly in divergent thinking, creativity, early metalinguistic awareness and communicative sensitivity'. This is a good reason to support children's first languages in school. A further reason to support the home language is because the learning of children who are acquiring English may suffer if they can only learn through the medium of a language in which they are not proficient. Their capacity to use language as a tool for thought continues in their first or other languages, but will take time to develop in the additional language. Practitioners can support children's learning through their first language by:

- recognizing and celebrating children's home languages;
- providing opportunities for children to hear their home languages through the use of audio and video materials;
- employing bilingual tutors or other support;
- inviting community members to work alongside children; and
- encouraging children who speak the same language to play and work together.

Language difficulties

Hearing impairment

Not all children develop language easily, although most children do. Children with a hearing impairment may have limited understanding and use of language. 'Almost 9 million people in the UK, one in seven of the population, suffer from deafness or experience significant hearing difficulty' (Deafness Research UK, 2005). For most children, hearing impairment is temporary and is caused by a build-up of wax in the ear, a condition that is often called glue ear. Other children will have a permanent hearing loss. It will probably be necessary to seek help from speech therapists and specialist teachers to support the language development of such children, and staff may need help in interpreting and putting an individual education plan into practice. However, there are some things that practitioners can do to support hearing-impaired children.

- Speak clearly and at a reasonable pace, but do not over-enunciate as this makes lip-reading difficult.
- If children have a hearing aid, make sure that it is switched on.

- Allow children more time to respond to questions and in discussions as it can take longer to process lip-reading.
- Make sure that hearing-impaired children can see the speaker's face and mouth.
- Make it easier for children to hear by having a quiet classroom.
- Use facial expression and gesture to convey your message.
- Keep what is said simple and be prepared to repeat what you say.

Reluctant talkers

In school, often when in large groups led by an adult, some children appear reluctant to speak. It is worth observing such children in a range of situations to see if they talk in the playground or when with small groups in the classroom. Most apparently quiet children are often articulate and confident in informal situations or when operating in a small group. This may lead teachers to ask themselves why children are reluctant to talk in some circumstances. It may be that children believe that in school teachers ask questions that have right answers and so it may be that a fear of getting it wrong deters some children from participating in discussions. Some children may be self-conscious about the way they speak. Unwittingly, adults may signal to children that short oral responses are what are required at school and so chidren get the message that teachers do not really want children to contribute very much. If the classroom organization or ethos is responsible, this can easily be changed. If children lack confidence then use puppets, masks or role play to allow them to talk for someone else. Giving children talk partners and asking them to relay what their partner has said fulfils the same function. Encouraging children to talk about something that they feel confident about, such as a hobby or an interest, will put them in the position of expert. Finally, some children are quiet and they have a right to be. Quiet children may be listening and thinking about what is being said, and so may be learning effectively.

Poor listening skills

It is not uncommon for adults to say that children today cannot listen. This is unlikely to be true. Children have learned to speak through listening to others and most children are adept at hearing things which adults might not want them to. Most children, like adults, are selective listeners and may find it hard to listen passively for long periods but they will listen attentively to things which interest them. Visual prompts and artefacts can be helpful in supporting listening and keeping young children's attention. Children may have difficulty in concentrating in a large group but listen well in a smaller group. Teachers need to keep periods when children are listening short and to build in opportunities for children to respond. The *Curriculum Guidance for the Foundation Stage* (QCA, 2000b) suggests that children should develop as active listeners who can respond to what they hear through questions and comments. They need opportunities to do this with a range of speakers, including friends as well as adults.

Selective mutism

Some children who have developed normal speech at home choose not to speak when they start school. They may talk to other children but not speak to adults. Their silence may have its roots in their discomfort at being at school or being away from home. It is usually a symptom of unease, unhappiness or protest. It does not help if adults try to make these children speak and such pressure will just add to their anxiety. From time to time they should be invited to contribute or answer as they need to feel included but a non-response should be accepted. This is not a common problem, less than one child in a thousand is affected, but it is of relevance to early years practitioners as most cases occur between the ages of 3 and 5. For many selective mutes this is a phase that passes when they feel more secure and relaxed. If mutism persists for two months or more, professional help should be sought and the child may be treated through an individualized, graduated programme.

Literacy difficulties

Not all children can respond easily to activities or show their understanding and learning through recording, particularly in the early years when orchestrating all the skills involved in writing is particularly taxing. Children who are less comfortable or successful with writing can share their ideas and their understanding orally. It is important for practitioners to accept oral as well as written evidence of children's learning.

Gender

The characteristics of talk used by boys and girls often differ. Girls are usually more collaborative and use talk to support each other and to develop ideas together. Boys generally propose ideas, often use language dramatically and move on quickly without adding detail or developing their ideas. They seem to listen less well than girls. The talk repertoires of both boys and girls can be extended by planning the composition of groups and talk partners, and changing them from time to time. This will help children to learn different ways of interacting. Planning to make sure that all children participate in different types of activities across the whole curriculum helps to ensure that all children get an opportunity to use language in different ways. Adults need to be alert to the types of talk that children do not use or do not use well, and through conversation and participation in activities help them to develop all aspects of talk.

Teaching speaking and listening

Lessons from parents

Adults play a crucial role in developing children's talk. At home parents and other experienced speakers have created the conditions in which children's talk has flourished. Practitioners can learn from interactions that parents have with children and the ways in which they have encouraged children's oral language development. We know that adults make learning to talk a positive and rewarding experience for children. They:

- expect children to talk;
- reward even their most rudimentary attempts with smiles and praise;
- view progress in talk as an important milestone;
- provide models of speech for children;
- are delighted when children 'have a go';
- incorporate early words and two- and three-word utterances into more extended sentences;
- engage in real conversations with children; and
- take the lead from children by responding to and extending what they say.

Teachers can learn from parents by creating a positive and encouraging climate for talk in the classroom, giving oral language status, engaging in authentic conversations with children about shared experiences and providing children with models of oral language use including language for thinking as well as language for communication.

Creating a positive environment is particularly important. Expressing one's own ideas and thoughts in public or to an unfamiliar or knowledgeable audience can be intimidating even to a mature or confident user of language.

Activity

When do you most like talking? Do you ever find talking difficult? Are there some speakers that you enjoy listening to? Why? Can you use your own experiences to create favourable conditions in which young children feel confident in speaking and enjoy listening?

Adults often find it difficult to talk when:

- other people ridicule the way they speak;
- they do not know the people they are talking to;
- they feel that they do not know as much about the topic as others do;
- the other person is not listening;
- the other person is not interested;
- they lack confidence.

Children also find it difficult to express themselves freely or show what they can do if they feel uncomfortable. Consequently practitioners need to create conditions which make talking easy and minimize the conditions which make talking difficult.

The teacher's role

Teachers have a threefold role in developing children's oral language. They need to plan opportunities for talk, provide models of different types of speaking and listening, and respond to and develop children's contributions. There are examples of the sorts of activities that can be included in the planned oral language curriculum for the Foundation Stage later in this chapter, and planning sequences of activities that develop speaking and listening is explored in Chapter 8.

The adults that children come into contact with provide children with models on which children base their own behaviour. Consequently practitioners need to model the vocabulary and speech habits that they want them to learn. As well as providing models through their everyday use of language in the classroom, practitioners can provide demonstrations of particular uses and forms of language by:

- asking for information;
- describing an object;
- recounting an experience; and
- giving reasons for their opinions.

Good speech habits include being a good listener. Good listening is mod-elled and encouraged when:

- children are given attention when they are speaking;
- hesitant talkers are listened to until they finish; and
- children's contributions are respected.

In school, practitioners can, in their eagerness to prompt talk, make too many demands on children and ask too many questions that have one-word or right or wrong answers. When this happens adult–child talk begins to be more like an examination rather than a genuine conversation and we know that it is the natural conversations that have taken place between parents and children that have resulted in children's tremendous achievements in speaking and listening before they started at nursery or school. Adults can best support the development of children's language for communication and thinking when they engage in real conversations with children. These often take place as adults and children share a familiar and undemanding activity together. Undertaking the same activity as the children or playing alongside them provides an excellent context for authentic interactions where the child can instigate questions and topics. It is important to allow children the space to lead conversations as, when talking with adults, children's contributions tend to be longer when they are initiated by the child (Bruner, 1980). It is during sustained conversations with adults that children have the chance to develop their ideas just as adults do and it is this type of conversation that we should be aiming to have with children.

In the following example, Liz, a nursery practitioner, was leading a pizza-making activity. She had resourced the activity well. On the table there were bowls containing cheese, ham, pineapple, sweetcorn and tomatoes. She had made labels to accompany each of the toppings. She also had a circular pizza base which she had cut into four sections. Next to the preparation table she had placed a table and chairs taken from the home corner and hung a notice above them which said 'Pizza Parlour'. She gathered four children to work with her, asked them to wash their hands and helped them to put on aprons. What follows is the conversation that took place between Liz and the children.

> *Liz*: We're going to make pizzas. You're going to choose your toppings and put them on your pizza. Then, we'll cook them and you can eat them. Daniel, which topping do you want? We've got cheese, ham, pineapple, sweetcorn and tomato.
> *Daniel*: I want some cheese.
> *Liz*: You want some cheese. OK. Take some and put it on your base. Do you want anything else?

Daniel: No.

Liz: No. Just cheese. OK. Bianca, what toppings do you want?

Bianca: I want some cheese and lots of pineapple.

Liz: You want some cheese and lots of pineapple. I like pineapple too. Tom, which toppings do you want?

Tom: I want pineapple and ham and cheese.

Liz: Do you want anything else?

Tom: No.

Liz: Pat the toppings down so they don't fall off when we put the pizza in the oven. Jo, choose your toppings and put them on.

Liz then put the pizzas on a baking tray and put them in the oven. While she did this she described what she was doing and told the children that they would be able to eat the pizzas later.

This activity had the potential to stimulate some rich oral language. However it did not. Why did it go wrong? Liz forgot to set the scene for the activity. She made no mention of the pizza parlour. She told the children what they were going to make rather than asking them what they thought they were going to do. She did not introduce the toppings or draw the children's attention to the labels. Liz was focused on the production of the pizzas. She repeated what the children said and asked limiting questions rather than engaging in a natural conversation. It could have been so different. Imagine an alternative scenario.

Liz: Can anyone guess what we are going to make today? ... Why do you think that? ... Yes, we are going to make pizzas and you are going to choose toppings that you like. Who has had pizza at home? ... Mmm me too. We sometimes have pizza when I'm too tired to cook. What about going out for a pizza? Has anyone done that? ... Daniel, what makes a good pizza for you? ... Who else likes ham and sweetcorn? ... What about you, Jo? What do you like? ... OK. Help yourselves to your favourite toppings and put them on the base. Are there any toppings that you don't like? ... Tom, why don't you like tomatoes? ... Now we have to press the toppings down. Why do you think that is important? ...

In the spaces between Liz's questions and comments you can imagine the children's contributions and how they would explain, consider and use their out-of-school experiences to inform their suggestions. This would result in extended discussion where the children's contributions rather than being brief would be at least as great as those of Liz. Liz could have learned a great deal about the children, followed up their comments and engaged in some authentic conversations with them had she not been so product focused, had she been interested in the children as individuals and had she opened up the conversation rather than closing it down.

> **Activity**
>
> Consider how you would conduct this activity. How would you introduce it to the children? What use would you make of the resources you had? Make a list of possible questions and conversation starters that you could use during the activity. To help you, you might think about how you would talk to a friend if you were doing some cooking together.

Activities to develop speaking and listening

Circle time

Circle time is generally a large group activity involving all or half of the class at a time. In turn the children are given the opportunity to say something about a topic that is of importance to them. They might suggest how the role-play area could be improved, propose the sorts of books that could be bought for the class library or share ideas about how resources such as the imaginative play area could be accessed more equitably. Their suggestions might be accompanied by reasons. Conducted in this way this activity enables children to engage in language for communication as they present and explain their own ideas and listen to what the other children say, and language for thinking by providing an opportunity for children to give reasons for their ideas.

Stories

Stories are a central part of the curriculum provision for communication, language and literacy, and offer opportunities for development in speaking, listening, reading and writing. As children listen to and share stories with others they are learning about the imaginative and creative use of words and the pleasures of language. The language structures that they hear can be explored and incorporated into their own use of language. Stories can be the starting point for discussions if children are invited to give their opinions on the stories that they hear. Their thoughts can be recorded in speech or think bubbles during shared writing and then displayed.

Games

Playing commercially made games or games made by staff or children provides opportunities for talking and listening. In particular they encourage turn-taking and repetitive forms of interaction which can be helpful for children who are developing English as an additional language. The two

Figure 2.2 *Game based on* Bet You Can't!

examples of games illustrated here are based on books. The first, Figure 2.2, was made by adults in the nursery and is related to *Bet you can't!* (Dale, 1987). This is a game for two children. Each child moves around the track in turn. If they land on a square containing something that has to be tidied away, they pick up a picture of that object and put it in their toy basket. The game ends when all the toys have been tidied away. When the children play this game they tend to use quite repetitive language, *I've got the rabbit*, *I've got lots of toys in my basket*, *It's my turn now*. But they might also talk to each other about the story and the toys they have at home.

The second game, Figure 2.3, was made by children and is based on *The Hunter* (Geraghty, 1994). The children worked in pairs with help from an adult to design their board game. They were shown an example of a track game and during shared writing they filled in some of the spaces using events from the story. Later they were provided with an open track to complete as they wished. Much of the talk came as the children worked together to make their game. They had to use language to communicate to 'interact with others, negotiating plans and activities and taking turns in conversation' as well as for thinking in order to 'organise, sequence and clarify thinking, ideas, feelings and events' (QCA, 2000b: 48 and 58). After completing their game the children had to explain how to play it to other children. They needed to be clear in what they said and to respond to any questions or misconceptions that the other children may have had. This provided the children with a real audience and a purpose for their talk.

Small-world play

Playing with puppets and sets of farm and wild animals and the dolls' house provides children with opportunities to create stories and experiment with creating scripts. To give greater structure to the children's story-making, the sand or water trolley could be resourced to reflect a story that the children are familiar with. For example, animal figures, a boat and a small human figure could be placed in the water trolley or a washing-up bowl so that the children could retell the story of *Mr Gumpy's Outing* (Burningham, 1978). Creating and re-creating stories helps children to use language for thinking as they 'use language to imagine and recreate roles and experiences' as well as fostering enjoyment in spoken language as they 'make up their own stories' (QCA, 2000b: 58 and 50). Activities that encourage children to revisit and reflect on books also help with reading, as they give children the opportunity to explore words and texts and gain an understanding of characters and plots.

Figure 2.3 *Game based on* The Hunter

Story props

Pictures of characters and objects can be cut out from favourite stories and laminated to form story props. They can then be used by children to retell familiar stories. Teachers can also use story props as they read stories to the class. This three-dimensional presentation of a story is particularly effective with children who are acquiring English as an additional language or children with visual or hearing difficulties as they provide extra clues about the important elements of the book that is being read and help children to identify the significant parts of the illustrations.

Listening centre

Tapes and CDs of stories, nursery rhymes and poems and non-fiction books can be placed with books and story props in the listening area. This provides children with the opportunity to listen attentively and to join in with the voice on the tape giving them the opportunity to engage with the language of different types of books and to enjoy rhythm and rhymes. The listening area can also contain telephones and a story-telling chair to prompt talk. Gillen et al. (2001) describe a great many ways of using telephones in the Foundation Stage including using them to speak to characters in books.

Story sacks

Story sacks (Griffiths, 2001) are large bags that contain a book and objects related to it. The objects can be used to retell and extend the book or just to play with and hold as the book is being read by an adult. A story sack related to *Handa's Surprise* (Browne, 1994) could contain a selection of plastic fruit or laminated photocopies of the illustrations of the fruit in the story, a basket, a non-fiction book about Kenya, an alphabet book such as *African Animals A B C* (Browne, 1995) or *Eating the Alphabet: Fruit and Vegetables from A to Z* (Ehlert, 1993), a doll dressed as Handa, a copy of *The Shopping Basket* (Burningham, 1980), which is very similar story to *Handa's Surprise*, some plastic animals and a set of colour words. This set of resources provides lots of stimulus for talk about books, characters, events in stories, familiar and unfamiliar experiences as well as prompting questions. Story sacks are often loaned to parents as they provide them with ideas and resources for lots of playful activities that help children to become familiar with books in enjoyable ways.

Media boxes

The idea of a media box (bfi education, 2003a) is similar to that of a story sack. The box contains a video of a film or television programme and a number of resources linked to the video. These might include a board game, role-play items, puppets, a book, recipes, interactive writing suggestions, resources for making models, play dough and action rhyme props. The boxes are available for parents and children to borrow. These stimulate conversation between adults and children at home and give children something to talk about at school.

Songs and rhymes

These encourage children's interest in language and develop their understanding of rhythm and rhyme. When children join in with actions as well as words they are fully involved and need to listen attentively. Listening to and clapping along with music also develops children's listening abilities. It is easy to make up songs and rhymes with children. For example, 'Mr Gumpy had a boat' could be sung to the tune of 'Old MacDonald had a farm'. Instead of the animals on the farm, the song will include the animals who get onto the boat.

Role play

Creating ingenious or realistic settings for imaginative play, such as a magical forest or a library, can stimulate a lot of talk between children. Adults in role can provide children with models that will help children extend their repertoire of talk and prompt their use of language for thinking as they use language to imagine and re-create roles and experiences. Adult involvement in role play is crucial in order to prevent the children's play and their use of language from becoming repetitive. Adults can engage in dialogues with children and through conversations encourage children to develop their ideas, sustain their talk and collaborate with others. Role-play areas can be created outdoors as well as inside. For example, to re-create the setting for *We're going on a bear hunt* (Rosen, 1989) a wooden plank could be used as a bridge, the climbing frame as a mountain, tyres as the sticky swamp and the sandpit as a desert.

Dressing up

Providing children with a range of hats and costumes for dressing up has a similar effect to creating imaginative play areas. The costumes prompt children to take on new roles and use language that is appropriate to the character they become. In addition to clothes, children can be provided with face masks or they can make these themselves. Animal masks related to the characters in *Mr Gumpy's Outing* (Burningham, 1978) could be used by a group of children to act out the events of the story using dialogue inspired by John Burningham. Using stories in this way gives children a structure to follow but also allows them the freedom to develop it in their own way.

Photograph books

Photographs of activities that the children undertake can be mounted in books and used as a prompt for the children to recall and relive their experiences. They are an excellent stimulus for talk for thinking. It is possible to get photograph albums that have a built-in audio recorder. Children can record their own description of the events in the photograph and these can be played back and listened to by others. Using tape recorders can help children recognize the need to speak clearly.

Pictures and objects

Pictures of objects taken from odd angles or unusual objects can stimulate speculation and reasoning as children attempt to identify the object. They may need an adult to prompt their thinking by asking: *What could it be? What does it look like? What does it feel like? Does it remind you of anything? Could it be used for anything?* The children's thoughts and suggestions could be recorded in speech bubbles and displayed around the picture or object before its true identity is revealed.

Other people

Visitors who are invited to talk to children about their job, their memories or their experiences provide children with opportunities to listen carefully and to ask questions. Along with visitors who read stories to children they can provide enriching language experiences as they may introduce children to different accents and dialects.

Reflecting on talk

Speaking and listening skills improve when we reflect on our use of language. Young children can be offered the opportunity to consider how they talk and to develop their awareness of the uses of oral language and how it can be adapted to suit different situations and audiences. The adult may start a discussion about speaking and listening by asking children questions such as: *Who do you like talking to? When do you like talking? When don't you like talking? Are you good at talking? How do you know? When is it hard to talk? Can you remember learning to talk?* Initially the children's answers may be quite brief but, if adults share their own experiences as users of language with the children and foster an atmosphere of reflection, the children will begin to think more seriously about language and to value speaking and listening.

Talking about work

During small-group or whole-class time at the end of sessions or in plenaries, children can be asked to reflect on their experiences and activities. They can be asked to consider what they have done today, what they have enjoyed, what they found difficult and what they might like to do tomorrow. Talking about their immediate experiences provides a context for talk and encourages children to use talk to clarify their ideas and feelings, and to categorize and organize their experiences.

Group work

Bruner (1980) suggested that the most sustained and productive conversations come from pairs of children working or playing together. In nursery and reception classes children are given many opportunities to play together, for example, in the sand and water trays, with construction materials or with small-world toys. In these situations children exchange and develop their ideas about the play. They often listen to each other and build on each other's suggestions. This is a productive forum for speaking and listening that is not dependent on adult involvement.

News

During news times children talk about something important that they have done or about something they have brought to show the class. This is often best done in a small group or, if the children are in a large group, they can talk and then listen to their response partner. Others members of the small group, or the response partners, should ask questions and make comments on what they hear. It is far easier to do this in a small group. Talking to an audience in this way encourages children to 'speak clearly and audibly with confidence and control and show awareness of the listener' (QCA, 2000b: 54). Selected items of significant news can be recorded in a large class news book. At the end of each half-term it is always fascinating to look back on what has happened to class members, and children enjoy looking at their own and others' contributions.

Projects

Topics such as 'Ourselves' or 'The Senses' are commonly explored in the early years. These provide a good opportunity for children to think about and undertake all sorts of activities related to listening. These could cover all curriculum areas and might include going on a listening walk, making musical instruments, making collages related to loud and quiet sounds, recording rhymes and creating a whispering tent in the room in which a range of resources that prompt listening, such as musical instruments that make quiet sounds, large seashells and tapes of peaceful music, could be placed.

Conclusion

Speaking and listening plays a major part in children's lives, enabling them to operate socially and develop cognitively. It is a key part of the curriculum for communication, language and literacy in the Foundation Stage or, as was stated in the Bullock Report (DES, 1975: 10.30), 'we cannot emphasise too strongly our conviction of its [oral language's] importance in the education of the child'. This sentiment has been echoed more recently:

> The indications are that far more attention needs to be given, right from the start, to promoting speaking and listening skills to make sure that children build a good stock of words, learn to listen attentively and speak clearly and confidently. Speaking and listening, together with reading and writing, are prime communication skills that are central to children's intellectual, social and emotional development. (Rose, 2006: 3)

 Further reading

Goodwin, P. (ed.) (2001) *The Articulate Classroom: Talking and Learning in the Primary School*. London: David Fulton.
This is a collection of chapters in which different authors explore how speaking and listening can be learned and taught throughout the primary age range. A number of chapters examine the practical aspects of organizing for talk in the Foundation Stage.

Paley, V.G. (1981) *Wally's Stories*. London: Harvard University Press.
The illustrations in this book show how sensitive and genuine interactions between adults and children enable young children to demonstrate their knowledge and develop their understanding.

Sharp, E. (2005) *Learning through Talk in the Early Years: Practical Activities for the Classroom*. London: Paul Chapman Publishing.
This book contains lots of practical ideas for developing speaking and listening in the Foundation Stage and Key Stage 1.

Chapter 3

Reading

Introduction

Practitioners in the Foundation Stage help children as they take their first steps towards becoming fluent readers. Learning to read can be hard as it involves learning and making use of a number of skills. It is important to make this journey as pleasurable, satisfying and easy as possible by supporting children, giving them engaging texts and worthwhile activities. Throughout the Foundation Stage we want children to recognize that reading is a pleasurable and worthwhile pursuit. This chapter describes how this might be possible and offers suggestions for working with children in enjoyable ways.

Fluent reading

Skilful and fluent readers can read and do read. They know how to read a range of different types of texts using a variety of strategies. They can apply phonic strategies, word recognition, grammatical knowledge, the meaning of the text and their knowledge of the world and life experience as they read in order to get pleasure and information from texts. They are able to apply their knowledge of how to read flexibly according to what they are reading and their purpose for reading.

When reading difficult texts about unfamiliar topics such as official documents, readers are likely to skim through the whole text, reading quickly to get an overview of the content. They may scan the text for key words and dates. They may then judge that the text requires a more careful reading as the information that it contains is important. If the text contains unfamiliar or technical vocabulary, readers might draw on their knowledge of phonics to sound out difficult words and consider what these mean by drawing on their understanding of the text. They will also be reading some words quickly as they use their ability to recognize whole words on sight. Their knowledge of how sentences are constructed supports their word recognition and their understanding of the text. Parts of the text might not be pertinent to their needs and so can be skipped; other parts might need to be read again before they are fully understood.

This kind of reading contrasts with how fluent readers who read fiction for pleasure engage with a novel. Most readers will read novels quickly or steadily. They will have selected the book because it appeals to them and will already have an idea of the content. There is no need to read through quickly and then reread. In general they know what to expect from such a text and will only rarely encounter unfamiliar words. They will use a range of strategies to recover the literal meaning of the text but their application will almost be unconscious. However, they will be looking for meanings beyond the literal. They will be interpreting the author's meanings and intentions, and evaluating and responding to what the author has written.

Adults who work with children in the Foundation Stage have the exciting job of contributing to children's journey towards fluent, purposeful, satisfying and independent reading. In the description of fluent adult reading we can see that readers need to know three main things about reading, and these are the main components of the reading curriculum in the Foundation Stage. Fluent readers know and children will need to learn about:

- the purposes for reading;
- how to read; and
- different types of texts.

Purposes for reading

Children do not enter nursery or reception classes without any understanding of the important role reading has in people's lives. They will have seen people reading in their homes, on the television and in their communities. They will have noticed adults or older siblings reading many different types of texts including bills, letters, greetings cards, catalogues, packaging, computer screens and text messages. Outside the home they may have seen people reading street signs, logos, posters, shop signs, tickets, maps, writing on buses or buildings. The number of texts that we encounter and read almost incidentally every day is enormous. There are also deliberate acts of reading such as reading books, magazines, newspapers and instructions. Children will have seen adults reading intently and carefully in order to find something out, they will have seen adults smile or grimace as they read and they will have heard adults talk about what they have read, from exchanging information about special offers in the supermarket to commenting on the novels that they are reading. From these models of readers and reading behaviour children will have observed that the act of reading has many purposes. It provides information and pleasure, and it is a useful and significant part of everyday life.

Practitioners can continue to make the uses of reading explicit to young children in everyday activities and routines, and in the planned curriculum for communication, language and literacy. The classroom environment provides children with lots of examples of writing that are useful and relevant to those who work there. There are displays, labels and notices on walls, resources and play areas. These generally provide information and are often referred to and read by staff. The role-play area may contain newspapers, comics and magazines as well as other texts. One of the most important pieces of writing that children will read everyday is their name on their coat peg and work tray. It is important to children that they are able to identify their own name and distinguish it from the names of other children so that they can claim their own space within the classroom.

Classrooms also contain areas dedicated to books and reading. These are usually comfortable places that signal the pleasure that books can bring. More importantly, the books that they contain are shared with children each day. Children come to associate books with stories and rhymes and can see that books contain material that can be enjoyed. Imaginative play areas and other planned activities are often linked to books that have been read to the class, and so children again associate books with fun. Books are referred to and displayed when topics are being explored by the class, and this demonstrates to children that books can be sources of useful information. The print-rich environment of early years settings shows children that books and reading are enjoyable, interesting and useful, and that reading has relevance to their everyday pursuits and interests.

Reading strategies

Concepts about print

During the Foundation Stage, children make a start on learning the reading strategies that will in time enable them to read independently. The first thing they need to know is how to go about reading, what Clay (1985) termed concepts about print or bibliographic information. They need to know that the front cover introduces us to the book, the back cover contains more information about the text and the author, and that once inside books have a starting page and a final page. They need to know that, in English, writing is arranged from left to right across the page and from top to bottom down the page. They need to realize that the author's words, which tell the same version of the story each time the book is read or contain the unvarying information, are located in the print rather than the illustrations. Allied to this, children need to recognize that illustrations provide readers with clues about the text and add to our understanding and enjoyment of what has been written. Finally, children need to realize that there is a relationship between oral and written language as what has been written can be said. However, the language in books is different to spoken language. It is usually written in complete sentences and may contain particular phrases such as *once upon a time* and use words that have been carefully selected for their impact, all of which are known as book language. Much of this knowledge is learned as children see adults handling books and as they watch while adults read to them. Adults sometimes deliberately teach directionality and oral and written language correspondence by running their finger under the words as they read them to the children, and teach children about the difference between print and illustrations by pointing to the pictures and to words as they are discussed.

There are four kinds of strategies that readers need to develop in order to be able to read well. These are:

- knowledge of context;
- grammatical knowledge;
- word recognition and graphic knowledge; and
- phonic sounds and spellings.

Knowledge of context

In reading knowledge of context involves:

- understanding the characteristics of different text types such as fairy tales or poetry;
- being aware of what the text is about, for example, families or school life;
- bringing background knowledge and prior experience of the world to the text in order to understand it;
- having an expectation that the text will make sense and that what has been written will make sense;
- using one's developing understanding of the text to continue to search

for the author's meaning and make informed guesses of words that are unknown; and

■ using illustrations to support one's understanding of the text.

In the *Curriculum Guidance for the Foundation Stage* being able to use knowledge of context is described as, '[Knowing] that print carries meaning [and] [Showing] an understanding of the elements of stories, such as main character, sequence of events, and openings and how information can be found in non-fiction texts to answer questions about where, who, why and how' (QCA, 2000b: 62). In the Foundation Stage contextual knowledge is taught and learned as adults share books with classes, groups and individual children. At story times or during shared reading sessions the adult will usually begin by telling the children the title of the book and discussing with them what the book might be about. The adult might ask the children to use the pictures to predict before the reading begins what might happen and to use their sense of how the story is unfolding and the illustrations to make further predictions at intervals during the reading. After a book has been shared with children there is usually a discussion about content and the characters, and the children might be asked to give their opinion of the story.

Activity

Imagine you are working with a child who seems to read without understanding. How could you change this?

Grammatical knowledge

Even very young children have an understanding of grammar. They know about word order in sentences and they know something about word classes. In Chapter 2 I described how young children's oral language development is characterized by an observation of the rules governing word order, which is in part dependent upon an understanding of parts of speech. For example, children might say *book gone* but they are unlikely to say, *empty gone*. Once children realize that written language shares many of the characteristics of spoken language, they can begin to use their awareness of language to predict or read unknown words in sentences. Adults often encourage this by pausing before words as they are reading aloud, maybe prompting children's guesses by using a question as in,

Adult reading: Jack climbed the beanstalk up to the giant's …
Adult asking: Where do you think the beanstalk led to?

Grammatical knowledge is reinforced when children observe adults writing and when they begin to experiment with writing themselves. Adults talk about writing complete sentences and ask for suggestions about words which could be included in a text that is being written. They are expecting children to offer grammatically appropriate words and will prompt children to offer words that will fit or words that will make sense. Applying their knowledge of grammar will be a very useful strategy when children begin to read more independently. Based on their knowledge of how language works, they will be able to make predictions of unknown words in a text.

Word recognition

Recognizing whole words is a reading strategy that children begin to develop early. Frith's research into reading (1985) revealed that children learn to recognize whole entities such as words by visual clues such as their overall shape and length. She suggested that this ability begins at about age 3 when children begin to recognize their own names and distinctive words and logos that are important to them. A number of research studies identifying the most frequently occurring words in written English have been done, most recently by Solity (2002). There is remarkable consistency between them. The hundred most common words account for approximately 50 per cent of all the words that pupils will need to read, and of these the first 16 account for approximately 25 per cent of all written words. Helping children to read these significant words will obviously be of benefit to young readers. This is recognized in the *National Literacy Strategy* (DfES, 2001a) where 45 high-frequency words that children should be able to recognize by the end of the reception year are listed. Children will encounter these words repeatedly in the books that are shared with them and this will help them to build up the number of words that they can recognize on sight. Activities such as matching games, word bingo (see Figure 3.3 later in this chapter), snap and book-based games such as those illustrated in Chapter 2 will give children more opportunities to see and remember key words.

Graphic knowledge

Graphic knowledge is the ability to recognize patterns in words and between words. Skilled readers recognize groups of letters as a whole as they read. If they see *ti* they expect to see these two letters followed by *on*. They recognize groups of letters such as *ing* as a whole unit. Graphic information also helps us to distinguish between words that are similar in length, shape and beginning and ending letters such as *hair* and *hear*. It also helps us make links between words such as *help*, *helper* and *helping*. This is a more sophisticated visual strategy than recognizing words as a whole based on the overarching appearance of a word, as it involves making fine visual distinctions.

During the reception year, children are expected to develop this ability through identifying letter strings in words that are introduced through early phonic work. This might involve children distinguishing onsets from rimes and generating lists of words which have similar rimes. Another way of helping young children to develop graphic knowledge is to explore and collect words that are related to the spelling of their own name, such as *Josh*, *gosh*, *posh* or *Josh*, *ship*, *shop*, *sharp*. Although these activities can show children that there are words that contain patterns which both look and sound alike, they can also reveal that there are words that look alike but that sound differently such as *head* and *bead*. Graphic knowledge has a beneficial effect on children's spelling as it encourages them to look carefully at words and build up a repertoire of letter combinations that occur frequently in words.

Phonics

In reading, phonic knowledge is the ability to use the association between letter sounds and letter shapes to read words which are not recognized on sight. It is an important reading strategy but, as the preceding sections in this chapter have indicated, it is not the only one because 'successful reading and writing will involve bringing together information from a range of sources, semantic, grammatical and grapho-phonic' (Beard, 1998: 32)

Phonics in the early Foundation Stage

Phonic skills such as letter identification, segmenting and blending, start to be taught in the reception year. In nursery classes phonics has a much broader meaning and encompasses activities such as playing with environmental and vocal sounds, rhyme, rhythm and alliteration, as these are crucial to nurturing the phonemic awareness necessary for learning to read and spell. At this stage there is little emphasis on matching sounds and letters; the emphasis is on developing phonological awareness. The activities in the early part of the Foundation Stage prepare children for the more systematic teaching and learning of phonics in reception.

In order to learn to speak young children have listened carefully to the sounds in their environment, distinguished between spoken language and other sounds, and have made fine distinctions between spoken sounds in order to distinguish between and use similar sounding words such as *cat* and *hat*. Early phonic activities in the nursery provide children with opportunities to continue to explore and play with sounds and language. Early activities promote good listening and looking, awareness of rhyme and rhythm, and encourage children to talk about sounds. Much of the learning at this stage will come from joining in with familiar songs and rhymes, playing with musical instruments and listening to sounds in the environment. Towards the end of the nursery year and at the beginning of the reception year practitioners will begin to help children understand that words consist of phonemes and that those sounds are represented by letters.

Activities to promote enjoyment of rhyming and rhythmic activities

- Listen to and join in with familiar songs and rhymes.
- Act out and saying nursery and action rhymes.
- Dance to familiar songs.
- Sing counting rhymes.

Activities to distinguish one sound from another

- Make a listening list of all the sounds that can be heard in the outdoor area.
- Use voices to re-create sounds heard on a listening walk.
- Make musical instruments with a range of sounds.
- Identify the sound cues on a computer programme.
- Record different sounds onto tape.
- Join in with sounds and animal noises in stories.
- Make sounds with water and resources in the water tray.
- Use voices in different ways such as to whisper, sing and growl.

Activities to show awareness of rhyme and alliteration

- Make alliterative phrases or sentences such as dizzy duck, laughing Lucy.
- Identify the common initial letter in a group of objects.
- Sort names and name cards using initial letters.
- Draw attention to alliterative phrases in nursery rhymes and songs.
- Play word games such as 'I went to market and I bought a car, some curtains ...'.
- Read rhyming stories to children such as those by Dr Seuss and Lynley Dodd.
- Have rhymes on tape available for children to listen to.

- Make up rhyming couplets with children: 'I like Mog, Mog likes dogs, I like mice, Mice are nice'.
- Spot the deliberate mistake in a rhyme such as 'Little Bo-Peep has lost her cats'.
- Set up a rhyme table.

Activities to recognize rhythm in spoken words

- Clap out the number of syllables in children's names.
- Repeat a single name or combine two names to create a rhythm.
- Clap to the rhythm of songs and rhymes.
- Make up additional lines to known songs which maintain the same rhythm.
- Use musical instruments to mark the beat in songs.
- March, walk or stamp in time to music.

Activities to continue a rhyming string

- Find words to rhyme with children's names, such as Mark, dark, lark, park.
- In turn, children think of a real or nonsense word that rhymes with a chosen word.
- Make a group rhyme based on a patterned text:
    Aunty Pat has a flowery hat.
    Uncle Bill climbs up the hill.
    Aunty Mary is small and hairy.
- Play rhyming Kim's game using a set of objects or pictures that rhyme.
- Read rhymes and rhyming stories to children such as those by Nick Sharratt or Colin and Jacqui Hawkins.

Activities to hear and say the initial sound in words and know which letters represent some of the sounds

- Use the children's names as a starting point for alliterative sentences: 'Harry likes ham and hamsters'.
- Send children off to play by using initial letters in their names.
- Children sort a group of objects according to the initial phoneme.
- Play I spy using a group of objects and saying all the phonemes in the word, for example c-u-p.
- Play I spy with a limited set of words, for example 'I spy part of my body beginning with n'.
- Fish for letters related to children's names in the water tray.
- Sing alphabet songs.

> ## Activity
>
> A practitioner was reading nursery rhymes to a group of children. She missed out the last word of each line and the children called it out.
>
> 'Try this one,' she said 'Humpty Dumpty sat on a fence!' The children called out the correct word.
>
> A few children made up their own examples for others to hear.
>
> Later the children were shown rhymes in a big book. They identified the rhyming words and tried to think of other words that rhymed with them.
>
> What other ways can you think of to help children enjoy nursery rhymes? How could you extend this activity?

By the end of nursery and at the beginning of their time in reception, children will have had opportunities to play with sounds in a range of contexts. The activities that they have experienced will have helped to develop their awareness of speech and other sounds, rhythm and recognition of rhyme and alliteration. They will have begun to develop the language to talk about sounds. They may be aware of some sound to letter correspondences such as the first letter of their names. This early phonological development has taken children from an awareness of syllables via rhythmic activities, to an awareness of onsets and rimes within syllables via rhyming and alliterative activities, to becoming aware of some initial phonemes in important words.

Phonics in the later Foundation Stage

At this stage, phonic skills consists of gaining:

- an understanding that words consist of phonemes;
- an understanding that phonemes are represented by graphemes;
- an understanding that a phoneme can be represented by one letter or more than one letter;
- an understanding that there can be more than one way to represent a phoneme;
- a knowledge of phoneme–grapheme correspondences;
- the skill of segmentation which helps with spelling; and
- the skill of blending which helps with reading.

There are approximately 44 sounds or phonemes in English and these are represented by 26 letters in about 140 combinations. Learning all 44 sounds and the ways in which they can be written will take children until the end of Key

Stage 1. In England, children are expected to be able to hear and say initial and final sounds in words and short vowels within words and link sounds to letters by the end of the Foundation Stage. They are also expected to be able to use segmenting and blending skills and phoneme–grapheme knowledge to read and spell regular, consonant vowel consonant, words (DfES, 2001a).

> Segmentation means hearing the individual phonemes within a word ... In order to spell a word, a child must segment it into its component phonemes and choose a grapheme to represent each phoneme.
>
> Blending means merging the individual phonemes together to pronounce a word. In order to read a child must recognize ('sound out') each grapheme, not each letter (e.g. 'th-i-n' not 't-h-i-n'), and then merge the phonemes together to make the word. (DfES, 2004b: 16)

Playing with Sounds (DfES, 2004b) suggests that the phoneme–grapheme correspondences for reception are introduced in six groups:

Group 1 s m c t g p a o.
Group 2 r l d b f h i u.
Group 3 v w y z j n k e.
Group 4 ll ss ff zz.
Group 5 sh ch th wh.
Group 6 ck ng qu x.

These have been grouped according to usefulness, ease of discrimination and development of handwriting. The daily phonic programme for reception pupils should consist of two or three activities each day. One should be on segmenting, the second on blending and a third on practising phoneme–grapheme correspondences. It is suggested that children spend about three weeks on each group of phonemes. At the end of the reception year, children will begin to use their skills in blending and segmenting to read and spell words containing consecutive consonant phonemes, for example *spot* or *list*, and use their knowledge of phoneme–grapheme correspondences to read some two-syllable words.

In the later Foundation Stage the suggestion is that children follow a structured phonics programme such as that outlined in *Playing with Sounds* (DfES, 2004b) or *Progression in Phonics* (DfES, 2001b) or a commercial scheme such as Jolly Phonics, THRASS, Superphonics, POPAT or Phonographix. One of the most important aspects of phonic work at this stage is that children should have the chance to apply their phonic knowledge and use it in their reading and writing.

Resources such as plastic and magnetic letters, small whiteboards and letter fans are useful resources to use with children as they undertake phonic activities. Games such as letter bingo, snap, letter dominoes, matching games with rhyming pictures and words and alphabet jigsaws will all help to reinforce phoneme–grapheme correspondences. Oral games such as I spy and The Minister's Cat, and continuing to read rhymes and rhyming stories as well as sharing alphabet books, will also help.

Young children using reading strategies

The illustration (Figure 3.1) of an adult sharing a book with 4-year-old Mollie at the beginning of her reception year shows how, even at this early stage of her reading development, Mollie is able to draw on a number of reading strategies to actively engage with words, illustrations and the meaning of the whole text. Her comments are shown in the speech bubbles. This base will be built on throughout her time in the Foundation Stage. The book that is being read to Mollie is *I Forgot* by Dyan Sheldon (1988). It is the story of a very forgetful little boy who finally remembers one very important thing.

Reading Stages

Introducing children to reading

It is never too early to introduce children to books and reading. Earlier in this chapter I described how children will become aware of print and reading in their homes and communities just as they notice other routines and objects in their environment. There are also studies of children who have been read to from a very early age, most notably the story of Cushla (Butler, 1979) a child who was born with multiple handicaps. For her and her family, books were a solace and a productive shared activity that led to Cushla's fascination with print and understanding of stories. There have also been other larger-scale projects that have shown the beneficial effects of sharing books with babies (Wade and Moore, 1993; 2000).

Emergent readers

There might be considerable variation in the extent of experience children have had with print, books and reading before they start nursery. Even

Jake was in a hurry this morning.

Said, 'e and i are in my name'.

He put on his clothes.

He brushed his teeth.

Joined in with teeth, was able to predict this from the pictures.

But he forgot one thing …

Mollie's comments show that she:
- Has some graphic knowledge
- Uses grammatical knowledge
- Uses the context provided by the illustrations.

'Oh, Jake,' called his mother as he rushed from the house. 'What about your shoes?'

Looked at the illustrations and said, 'his toe's come out there's a hole in his sock'.

Jake jumped on his bike and raced to the shops.

He counted his change.

Counted 1, 2, 3.

He even remembered to check his parcels before he left each shop. He only forgot one thing …

Mollie's comments show that she:
- Is involved in the story
- Is looking carefully at the illustrations
- Is using her own experience to add detail to the story.

'Oh, Jake,' said his mother when he ran into the house. 'Don't tell me you came back without your bike.'

Joined in here but substituted basket for bike. Jake is holding a basket in the illustration.

Mollie's comments show that she:
- Is confident enough to 'have a go'
- Is able to make a grammatically appropriate substitution.

Jake had something to do in the garden.

> Looked at the pictures and talked about them before the adult began reading.

He remembered to put on his boots.

He remembered to put on his mother's gardening gloves.

> Repeated the last word of each sentence as it was read to her.

Mollie's comments show that she:
- Wants to read and is highly motivated
- Is enjoying the book and is involved in the story.

Jake had something to wrap in a hurry.

He got out the paper and the scissors.

He got out the sticky tape and the basket of ribbons.

The only thing he forgot about was the cat …

> Pointed to the picture of the cat and said 'There's the cat! He's going to make a mess.'

Mollie's comments show that she:
- Can read the illustrations
- Can predict what will happen.

'Oh, Jake!' yelled his mother. 'Now look what you've done.'

'Surprise! Surprise!' he shouted when she opened the door. 'Happy birthday! Happy birthday! Happy birthday!'

'Oh, Jake,' laughed his mother. 'And I thought you forgot.'

> Said, 'He didn't. First time he didn't.'

Mollie's comments show that she:
- Has understood the story, the character of Jake, the humour and the point of the repetition.

Figure 3.1 *Mollie reading* I Forgot

those with significant experience are unlikely to have well-developed reading strategies, although they may be in a good position to swiftly acquire a range of reading behaviours. But at this stage all children are learning quickly and, through the models, teaching and planned opportunities for exploration and learning, all children can make rapid progress in emergent reading.

During the ages of 3 and 4 we first want children to:

- understand the purposes and pleasures of print and reading;
- understand the organization of books and how books work;
- understand how to use books by turning the pages, moving from the front to the back of the book, reading the pictures and looking at the text;
- understand that reading is connected to writing and speaking;
- recognize familiar logos such as those for supermarkets, restaurants or toys;
- recognize their names;
- recognize some letter shapes;
- begin to recognize language patterns in songs, stories and books; and
- demonstrate reading-like behaviour when they return to familiar books by using clues from the illustrations and their memory of the story to retell the book and act like the adult readers they have seen and heard.

We then want them to move on and show that they are beginning to:

- track print from left to right across a line of print;
- return their eyes to the beginning of a second line of print;
- develop phonemic awareness by becoming aware of sounds in spoken language;
- recognize that print is made up of individual words;
- match the voice to words in a line of text;
- understand that words consist of a collection of letters; and
- understand that letters represent sounds.

At this stage children need many opportunities for listening to books being read aloud. They need 'reading demonstrations' (Smith, 1994) with adults reading to and with children individually and in large and small groups using enlarged texts, books chosen by adults and books chosen by children. These books need to be shared many times and be available for children to read alone or take home to share with parents so that children can become sufficiently familiar with them to enjoy retelling them to themselves and others. Readings will be followed by discussion about the books, the characters and the events. The children will be encouraged to give their opinions about what they have heard and to relate the story to their own experiences.

Beginning readers

During the reception year most children will begin to use more reading strategies. Their attempts at reading show that they are now able to focus much more on the text and rely less on memory or illustrations. They are able to match a word in print with its spoken equivalent and may use their finger to point to help as they read. They will still find it difficult to tackle unfamiliar texts independently and so need to continue to share and talk about many texts with adults or more experienced readers. At this stage a structured but age appropriate phonic programme usually begins.

Beginning readers begin to draw on:

- knowledge of the patterns of oral language (grammatical knowledge);
- memory of words or phrases which they heard during shared or paired reading (word recognition);
- support from the illustrations (knowledge of context);
- knowledge of sounds (phonics);
- recognition of patterns in words (graphic knowledge);
- understanding of the world (knowledge of context);
- knowledge of how books work (concepts about print); and
- a desire to make sense of what they read (knowledge of context).

As children reach the end of this stage they will be making increasing use of contextual, grammatical, graphic and phonic strategies to read unfamiliar words. Their experience of the world, the illustrations and their familiarity with the text from having heard it read to them guide their attempts to work out what would make sense. Their knowledge of syntax can tell them what sort of word would fit into a sentence. Their graphic and phonic knowledge encourages them to use what they know about letters and sounds to produce a best fit for the unknown word. Using one strategy or, better still, all the strategies enables children to narrow down the options for the word that they are trying to read.

Developing readers

At this stage, children are on their way to being able to read independently. Most children will reach this stage during Key Stage 1 but some able readers may reach this stage towards the end of the reception year. They are becoming less dependent on adult support and will not need to have heard the book read to them before they try to read the text themselves. They will have developed an extensive sight vocabulary, use a range of reading strategies, reread phrases or sentences when they are stuck and self-correct. They may begin to read silently. They will benefit from discussing the content of the book before they read and using information from the cover and any previous experience they have of the author's other books when they read. It is helpful to identify and discuss new and potentially difficult words as well as unfamiliar character and place names before they begin to read alone.

Selecting books and texts

Throughout the Foundation Stage adults will be introducing children to books that draw them into reading and that extend their developing awareness of print. For the most part adults will be sharing picture books with children. Not all picture books are simple reads and so it is worth trying to separate picture books into levels of difficulty that match the reading stage that children have reached. There are some common principles which guide the selection of all books to include in a collection for the early years, and these include:

- books that are well written;
- books that are well illustrated;
- books that offer memorable reading experiences;
- books that reflect a variety of backgrounds and cultures; and
- a collection that contains variety in content and style of illustration.

Books for babies and toddlers

Any books can be shared with babies but there are some types of books such as board books, cloth books, bath books and books to touch and explore that are particularly suitable. A number of authors such as Jan Ormerod, Helen Oxenbury, Shirley Hughes and Joyce Dunbar write about babies and toddlers. Their books often show very young children engaging in everyday activities such as eating, sleeping and playing with adults and siblings. The familiarity of these activities provides an ideal opportunity for adults and children to discuss the content of the books and make comparisons between the lives of the children in the stories and the lives of the readers. Other books that are suitable for this age group include nursery rhymes and songs and caption, counting and alphabet books.

Picture books for emerging readers

The ideal books for readers at this stage are those that can be read to children and which will support joining in during shared reading or retelling when children look at the book again either with an adult or independently. As these books will be read many times the story and the illustrations need to be sufficiently strong to keep the reader's interest and continue to be a source of pleasure when they are returned to.

Books for this stage should contain text that follows a pattern or is predictable. The predictability may come from the use of rhyme, rhythm, repetition of words or phrases or the use of familiar sequences such as the days of the week or numbers from 0 to 10. Examples of books include *Dear Zoo* (Campbell, 1984) and *Ten, Nine, Eight* (Bang, 1987). Illustrations which are closely linked to the text are helpful to young readers. Familiar rhymes or songs also make good reading material for emerging readers. The rhythm and the rhyme help children to remember the text and encourage them to join in with the repeated parts as the adult reads and support the child's efforts to retell the text later and read or make accurate predictions about words. They provide children with opportunities to behave like readers. Examples of books containing strong rhymes and rhythms include *The Wheels on the Bus* (Cook, 1998) and *Walking through the Jungle* (Lancome, 1993). Caption books encourage children to read the illustrations, and the text can help children read the words more accurately. For example, looking at a picture of a bird and then looking at the beginning letter of the caption which is *p* can guide the child's prediction away from *bird* towards *parrot*. Enlarged texts or Big Books are useful throughout the Foundation Stage and beyond as they provide children with a way of seeing as well as listening to the words when the adult is reading. Teachers can invite children to join in using visual cues provided by the text as well as those afforded by rhyme, rhythm, illustrations and memory.

Picture books for beginning readers

It should go without saying that the books we select for young readers should be well written and enduringly enjoyable if we want children to develop positive attitudes to reading. At this stage adults need to find books that children can read themselves after they have been read to them. Because we want children to begin to read more independently yet successfully, the texts will be fairly simple. They will probably be about familiar topics, such as home, family, friends and animals, and will have a limited number of words on each page, generally between one and ten. They will contain vocabulary that is familiar to them from their oral repertoire and simple sentence structures. Such simplicity need not be dull or unsophisticated as Pat Hutchins (1970) demonstrates in *Rosie's Walk*. Here a 32-word sentence is presented as a series of short phrases and clauses which tell at least two gripping and comic stories.

Throughout this stage children grow in confidence and ability, and as they progress they will be able to read books that contain an increasing amount of literary language, such as *said the rabbit, once upon a time* and *one day*, and vocabulary that might be outside the children's own experience. The books will have increasing amounts of text on each page maybe as much as four or five lines lines. Illustrations may no longer be directly linked to the text, and when two or more sentences occur on the same page the illustration may only support one of them. Typical books at this level include *The Doorbell Rang* by Pat Hutchins (1986) and *Mr Gumpy's Outing* by John Burningham (1978).

Books for developing readers

Young able readers need to continue to experience a rich diet of picture books. At this stage children need books that they will be able to read alone or with limited support after an initial discussion. If children are given material that contains too much text, too few illustrations and that is conceptually too difficult for a young child, they may begin to find reading a chore rather than a joy and be put off reading. There are sufficient numbers of picture books to provide young children with new experiences and to provide them with opportunities to consolidate their reading. Many books have been written to help adults make choices about books for children. One that is particularly suitable for practitioners in the Foundation Stage is *The Rough Guide to Children's Books 0–5* by Nicholas Tucker (2002). New children's books are also regularly reviewed in newspapers, magazines, journals and on websites written for those working in education.

Core books

Core books (Ellis and Barrs, 1996) are carefully selected collections of quality books that are used as a basis for organizing the literacy curriculum and teaching reading. School staff decide on the core collection of books that will be used by each class. This set of books will be read repeatedly to and by children over the year so it is important that they have an enduring appeal and are of high quality. The class collection will contain books from a range of genres including wordless books, picture books, poetry, joke books, traditional stories, contemporary stories, humorous stories, plays, novelty or interactive books and information books. Some of the books should be available as Big Books. The selection for each class should match the reading level of the children and be appropriate to their age and interests. Story props, games and story sacks are often made to accompany these books.

In the Foundation Stage, work across the curriculum is often planned in thematic blocks. It is very easy to make sure that books which can be used with the themes are included in the class core book collection. For example if Growth is a regular spring topic, books such as *Jasper's Beanstalk* (Butterworth and Inkpen, 1992), *Titch* (Hutchins, 1972) and *The Tiny Seed* (Carle, 1997) could be part of the collection and read to and by the children during the course of the theme. The range of books suggested in the *National Literacy Strategy* (DfES, 2001a) can also inform the choice of books to be included. For reception classes this would include traditional, nursery and modern rhymes, chants, action verses, poetry, stories with predictable structures and patterned language and recounts.

The reason for having a set of core books is that through frequent encounters with a limited number of books children will build up a repertoire of texts that they know well. During the initial stages of reading they will be meeting books that they already know and this enables them to achieve success and satisfaction with their early attempts. Children's familiarity with core books is built up through:

- reading them aloud to the children;
- having them available for independent, quiet reading;
- ensuring that they can be taken home to be shared;
- retelling the stories with story props;
- using core books for guided reading;
- using the books for shared reading; and
- doing shared writing based on the books.

Other activities can also be used to extend children's familiarity and understanding of core books, and these might include:

- making models;
- making collages;
- making displays;
- painting and drawing; and
- role play based on the books.

Reading schemes

Over the years, reading schemes as a resource for learning to read have had a bad press from many educationalists. They have been called 'unvaried' and 'uninspiring' (Solity, 2006) and dull and disconnected from the world of young children (Williams, 2001). Whitehead (2002) writes of the 'meaningless repetition' and 'very thin plot' found in many scheme books. In a report which stresses the need for pleasure in reading, Her Majesty's Inspectorate (HMI, 2004) describes reading schemes as restrictive and contributing to negative attitudes towards reading. Given all the wonderful books that have been written and illustrated for young readers, schemes seem unnecessary. Picture books can be read and reread, which is necessary for children who are learning to read, and these are the books that will engender a love of reading.

Environmental print

Foundation Stage classrooms need to contain a variety of printed material. The mainstay of the reading curriculum is likely to be books but if we are to signify the full range of purposes for reading then classrooms need to contain some of the real material that is found in children's homes and communities. Junk mail, newspapers, magazines, comics, bills, letters, greetings cards, leaflets, catalogues and packaging are a familiar sight in everyone's house in the twenty-first century. Street signs and notices, logos, posters, shop signs, tickets, writing on carrier bags can be seen every day in the locality that children inhabit.

Street signs and traffic signs can be incorporated easily into the outdoor play area. It is possible to buy or make 'Stop' and 'Give way' signs and bus stops and to paint or chalk 'Slow' and 'Keep clear' markings onto the ground. The wheeled vehicles can be given number plates. A garage can be set out outside with a variety of literacy materials such as bills, MOT certificates and posters that are commonly found in garages (Hall and Robinson, 1995). It might be possible to set up a market stall outside with a stall name, labels and price tags. This emphasis on using environmental print in the outdoor area could be combined with a topic that is helping children to find out about locality through visits, photographs and books – one of the key elements of the curriculum for knowledge and understanding of the world (QCA, 2000b).

Newspapers, magazines, comics, bills, letters, greetings cards, calendars, leaflets and packaging can be included in indoor imaginative play areas such as the home corner or various types of shops. Packaging and print from comics and newspapers can be used to make print games such as matching or snap games using logos from cereal packets. Children can cut out the letters in their names from printed materials, and resources such as alphabet friezes or alphabet books can be made using food wrappers or toy packaging. A sweet-wrapper alphabet is illustrated in Figure 3.2.

Aa Aero	Bb Bounty	Cc Caramel	Dd Dairy Milk	Ee Eclairs
Ff Flake	Gg Green & Black	Hh Heroes	Ii Iced Gems	Jj Jelly Babies
Kk Kit Kat	Ll Lion Bar	Mm Milky Bar	Nn Nougat	Oo Orange Cream
Pp Polo	Qq Quality Street	Rr Rolos	Ss Smarties	Tt Twix
Uu Ugly Tots	Vv Violet Creams	Ww Walnut Whip	Xx Chocolate Xtra	Yy Yorkie Zz Zingy Lime

Figure 3.2 *A sweet-wrapper alphabet*

Using environmental print offers practitioners a readily available resource for learning about what written language does in everyday contexts. It reflects children's experiences with print at home and in their communities, and provides continuity of language and literacy experience between home and school (Miller, 1999). It reflects the three strands outlined in the *Curriculum Guidance for the Foundation Stage*:

- provision for the different starting points from which children develop their learning, building on what they can already do;
- relevant and appropriate content that matches the different levels of young children's needs; and
- planned and purposeful activity that provides opportunities for teaching and learning both indoors and outdoors (QCA, 2000b: 11).

Media texts

The literacy curriculum needs to include challenges that are relevant to young children today. Even the youngest children have learned to read films, videos and television programmes and adverts (Marsh, 2005). Working with moving images can encourage reading at a level beyond the literal. It can help young children talk about their interpretation of the text, their responses to the text and to read critically. Activities related to age appropriate films, videos and television programmes can help children to talk about genre, setting, characterization and the development of the plot. The use of colour and music and the way characters are dressed or talk give us clues about good and bad characters, their intentions, danger points in the plot, complications and the resolution of the story. Children are and can become more adept at reading these signs. These features are characteristic of written texts and the ability to interpret what is happening and how we know in media texts can be transferred to reading printed texts. An example of planning using film as a starting point is given in Chapter 8.

Activity

Think about your own early experiences of reading. What was read to you and what reading material did you have access to and read? What are the earliest books you remember reading at school? What books have been influential in your life as a reader? What do you read now? Use your own memories of books to consider what reading material we should make available for young children.

Activity

You encounter a child who seems to lack interest in reading. What steps might you take to engage him or her?

Teaching reading

Reading stories aloud

Reading a story to a class or group of children is a pleasurable experience. The books that are shared are usually carefully chosen for their merit, their appropriateness to the children's interests and understanding, and their links to topics that are being investigated by the class. Many of the stories will be taken from the core book collection, which will contain a variety of genres and represent our diverse society. In nursery and reception classes favourite books will be reread and enjoyed many times.

Reading stories supports children's reading and language development in many ways. It shows children the pleasure and purpose of reading. It provides children with a demonstration of how to read. Through listening to stories children develop an understanding of stories. Their knowledge of vocabulary, written language and the way in which texts are structured is increased. Very importantly in the Foundation Stage, story reading gives children a bank of known stories that they can begin to read individually and with some independence once they are familiar with them.

Shared reading

In shared reading the adult normally reads an enlarged text to a large or small group of children. This enables the children to see and hear the words simultaneously and to join in the reading when they are familiar with the text. A variety of texts can be used in shared reading including stories, poems, songs, non-fiction and texts that have been written with the class by the teacher.

Like reading aloud, shared reading involves children in reading in enjoyable and purposeful ways. During the reading the teacher can demonstrate early reading strategies such as word by word matching, word recognition and prediction. Books are read many times and children are given opportunities to join in and behave like readers in a positive and non-threatening way as it is the group that is reading rather than the individual. Shared reading creates a body of known texts that children can use for independent reading, particularly if small versions of the book are available or if the enlarged text is placed in the reading area.

Guided reading

Guided reading is probably most suited to reception age children in the Foundation Stage. Here the teacher works with a small group of about four to six children who are at a similar reading level and have the same reading needs. Each child will read the same book that has been carefully matched to the group. The book may be new to the children or it might have been introduced through shared reading or a story-reading session. The teacher introduces the book and takes the children through each page so that the children get a sense of what the book is about. Any unfamiliar concepts are discussed and explained. Any potentially difficult vocabulary is identified and drawn to the children's attention. The children are reminded that they are going to read the book quietly to themselves and that there are a number of reading strategies – context, grammatical knowledge, word recognition, graphic knowledge and phonics – that they can use if they cannot read the words. As the children read, the teacher supports them if they encounter any difficulties. At the end of the session the teacher will make some teaching points about the application of reading strategies and the children and the teacher will discuss their understanding and response to the text. With very young readers the teacher might read with the children, as with shared reading.

Guided reading provides an opportunity for children to read a complete text. The children practice the use of all reading strategies with the help and support of the adult. They also have the opportunity to reflect on their use of reading strategies and the content of what they have read. It gives the teacher the chance to teach reading to the group and to individuals, and to assess children's progress and needs.

It is helpful to integrate guided reading into the planned weekly programme of activities for communication, language and literacy. This gives children the opportunity to revisit the book and consolidate some of their learning from the guided session. Children can be given follow up activities such as:

- listening to the story on tape;
- writing a letter to one of the characters in the story;
- retelling the story using small-world resources;
- acting out the story in the role-play area;
- reading the book to the dolls and soft toys in the reading area;
- sequencing the sentences taken from the book;
- incorporating ideas from the book into role play;
- matching words from the story with objects;
- making words from the story using word fans or plastic letters;
- retelling the story using story props;
- allowing the children to take the books home to read again.

Independent reading

Independent reading is a common feature of nursery and reception classes. It is a routine that can occur at transition times such as between tidying up time and going outdoors to play or when children return to class after lunch and are waiting for registration. It can also be an activity that is available at any time if children choose to use the reading area. Sometimes children will read alone during these times but they may choose to read with a partner.

This can be an opportunity for children to learn from each other. Building in times when children can read books independently allows them to revisit favourite books, behave like a reader, establish a reading habit and apply their reading strategies. At these times it is often possible for adults to support a child, to discover their reading interests and to observe their use of reading strategies. See Chapter 7 for an example of this.

Reading with an adult

At the early stages of learning to read, children are not able to read independently so rather than reading to an adult, adults will read to children. The books that are shared are maybe those in the core book collection or books that have previously been heard during shared reading or story sessions. As the adult reads the book there will be opportunities to talk about what is happening in the story and the illustrations, to predict what will happen next and to discuss characters, their feelings and motivation, and the child's opinions of the text. Reading to a child is a rich learning-to-read experience as children learn:

- how books work;
- what a story is;
- book language;
- to anticipate and predict;
- a sight vocabulary;
- that language is composed of separate words;
- about rhyme, rhythm, alliteration and repetition;
- to recognize letters;
- to engage with books; and
- to interpret and understand what is read.

After reading the book, the adult and child can retell the story using the illustrations as prompts. In time, after having had a number of books read to them a number of times, children will be able to retell familiar books using some of the language and words from the book. Later, as children become even more familiar with a book, they will start to join in as the adult reads, because they will recognize some words and phrases. Gradually the child's contributions will increase not only because they can remember more of the text but because their understanding of how to use more reading strategies increases as a result of the other literacy work that is going on in the class. When the child starts to join in more, the adult should be prepared to stop reading when the child is reading but be prepared to join in if the child falters or stops. It also helps to build up the child's confidence in their ability to read if the adult accepts the child's approximations of words if these maintain the sense of what is being read. Eventually the balance of responsibility for reading will change from the adult to the child and the child will begin to read much more independently. Even when this happens, the adult will still be there to introduce the book, supply unknown words and initiate a discussion about the book. The adult will also teach the child about reading after the book has been completed. Difficult words can be identified and read again or the child can be shown how to use phonic knowledge to help with unknown words.

It can be useful to have some prompts to initiate discussions about books and reading with children. Some helpful open questions include:

- What did you think when ... ?
- What would you do ... ?
- How do you think she felt ... ?
- Would you like to do that ... ? Why?
- Did you enjoy that?
- Which was your favourite part?

Paired reading

This often involves children of different ages reading together. In the Foundation Stage it can be beneficial to have older children reading to reception age children. This is another opportunity for young children to become familiar with and enjoy core books, and will contribute to their ability to join in when reading with an adult.

The literacy hour in reception and nursery classes

The additional guidance in the National Literacy Strategy framework (DfES, 2001a) says that the objectives for the reception year should be taught systematically from the beginning of the year. It also advises that some of the teaching methods such as shared reading and guided reading should be introduced from the start, although these need not form part of a literacy hour. The recommendation is that a full literacy hour should be introduced as soon as possible and by the end of the term before children move into Year 1 at the latest. Teachers are also encouraged to plan for shared reading and writing and regular sessions of guided reading with older nursery age children.

Reading activities and resources

Story props

Story props are pictures of the central characters and objects from a story. As the story is read or told, the pictures are placed onto a board or a story stick so that the children can see the characters and objects come to life. Story props are very helpful for children who are learning English as an additional language as they see a picture and hear the word which describes it without the possible confusion which may be caused by looking at the detailed illustrations in a book. Story props should be available for children to play with after they have been introduced by an adult. This allows children to retell the story in their own words or create a story of their own using the props and so gain further experience of the story and its key vocabulary.

Sometimes a collection of real objects can be used to support a story telling or story reading. For example, a pair of blue shoes, a black mac and a multicoloured scarf could be used with *The Green Queen* (Sharratt, 1992). Later, the children can use these in their play. With a group, small-world toys can be used to tell the story. This provides the children with a model that they can emulate later.

Role play

To provide children with another opportunity to explore stories, the role-play area can be resourced to reflect the setting of a book. For example, it could contain a rocket large enough for the children to sit in if *Whatever Next!* (Murphy, 1983) has been read to the children, or it could be furnished as the three bears' house. Masks and appropriate dressing-up clothes help the children to get into role. The props can be very simple, for example, a large cardboard box for Baby Bear's rocket, a green colander for his space helmet, and a pair of wellingtons for his space boots. Role play can also take place outside. A bridge constructed from wooden blocks and planks could be used to re-enact *The Three Billy Goats Gruff*.

Role play that helps children both to use reading and appreciate the uses of reading can take place in real-life settings that children are familiar with. It is very easy to set up a supermarket as the resources are readily available. Resources could include:

- food packaging;
- comics, magazines and newspapers;
- greetings cards;

- books;
- labels;
- price tags;
- special offer signs;
- food posters; and
- a community noticeboard.

Some of these resources can be made or added to by the children or created during shared writing sessions with an adult. This will help the children to read the signs when they are playing in the supermarket.

Painting characters

Painting or making collages of characters in books is a good way of encouraging children to return to a text that has been introduced earlier. In order to produce an accurate representation, children will need to check the sort of clothes the character wears, the colour of the clothes, the hairstyles and other details. Paired work on a collage can also stimulate talk about the character.

Speech bubbles

If the children have made large representations of characters, they can go on to make speech bubbles to go with these portraits. What might the character say? What would characters say to each other? This activity helps the children to explore further the idea of character.

Sequencing

Sequencing involves arranging a set of pictures or sentences, or both, in order. Although children can do this individually, it is often more productive for pairs of children to cooperate on a sequencing activity or for a small group led by an adult to put the cards in sequential order. When sequencing a set of pictures taken from a story, children are practising the language of the story. As they work together they are negotiating meaning, sharing ideas and developing their listening skills. Once the pictures are ordered the children should be able to retell the story and, with practice, may be able to use some of the author's original language. The children can also experiment with the cards to create their own version of the story. Sequencing activities using sentences taken from the story are more suited to the reception year group. Here the children have the opportunity to practise their reading in a playful activity. Sequencing activities can also be done with sets of photographs taken during an outing or a cooking or science activity. These will prompt children to use the language of non-fiction texts as they recall what they did.

Games

Games are an excellent way of helping children to learn about language and literacy as they provide an enjoyable and social context for learning. They can vary from simple games such as bingo, snap and pelmanism, to track, dice and sentence-matching games. Bingo, snap and pelmanism can be used to help children learn words that cannot be sounded out using phonic skills and so need to be recognized on sight. For this purpose the words that are used can be taken from the high-frequency word list (DfES, 2001a). For young children the number of words that are included in any one game should be limited. Each bingo card should have six words. Bromley (2000) suggests that, rather than just using isolated words on the bingo card, they can make a sentence or phrase from a story. This would foster reading for meaning as well as learning some key words. Both kinds of bingo are illustrated in Figure 3.3.

Dice games allow children to collect objects from a story. The *Bet you can't!* (Dale, 1987) game in Chapter 1 is a good example. These games need not be arranged on a track. For example, a game made to accompany *How do I put it on?* (Wantanabe, 1979) could consist of a large dice on which are written some key words from the story including cap, shirt, shoes, pants. The children collect the item of clothing that shows on the dice when they roll it, and dress a cut-out bear. Similarly, children could collect the animals who accompany Mr Gumpy on his outing (Burningham, 1978) and place them in a boat.

Track games such as that based on *The Hunter* (Geraghty, 1994) and illustrated in Chapter 1 can be made with a group of children. Thinking up the prompts to advance or go back necessitates re-reading the book and using the events. This helps children to think about story structure and encourages reading for meaning.

Story sacks

Story sacks (Griffiths, 2001) were designed to help adults share books with children in a way that is positive and interactive. Each story sack is related to a popular children's book. The story sack, a large cloth, drawstring bag, contains a number of items related to the chosen book. The collection of items related to the text and the suggestions for exploring the book further are intended to develop young children's interest in books and reading, and encourage them to reread or look at the book again. Through using the props, playing the book-related games with an adult, listening to the story and exploring the non-fiction text, children become familiar with a range of texts, explore different types of texts and build up a store of books that they can return to and look at and begin to enjoy alone.

look	are	we
and	on	like

What	big	teeth
you've	got	Grandma.

What	big	eyes
you've	got	Grandma.

Figure 3.3 *Base boards for sight word bingo*

A typical story sack might contain:

- a good quality story written for young children;
- toys representing the book's main characters;
- other props referred to in the text;
- scenery related to the setting of the book;
- an information book related to the content of the story;
- an audio tape of the story;
- an audio tape of the information book;

- a language-based game related to the story;
- examples of environmental print related to the story; and
- suggestions about how to make good use of the props and the games.

Story sacks were originally designed for parents and carers to use with children at home, and many schools and nurseries have a library of story sacks that can be borrowed usually for about a week at a time. This gives adults and children time to explore the contents of the sack thoroughly and become familiar with the books that it contains, particularly the story book. Many libraries and local education authorities have also developed their own stock of story sacks and these can be borrowed by schools and parents. Not all story sacks need to be sent home. They can be used by teachers as a classroom resource to support the teaching of language and literacy in school.

Practitioners can use the props, characters and scenery to bring a story-reading or story-telling session to life. They can then be used with the children to retell the story and to sequence the events. Retelling the story using props can encourage children to use story language and to develop and use their oral language. They may choose to use the characters as puppets and speak through them. The props can also be used to create new versions of the original story. The props can be used as a focus for discussing aspects of the books such as the setting and the characters. Story sacks may be particularly beneficial for children who are learning English as an additional language or for children with special educational needs. The props can provide visual support for the vocabulary and events in a story which is helpful to bilingual learners and children with hearing impairments. Children with visual impairments or physical difficulties can benefit from the opportunity to explore aspects of stories through touch.

The benefits of using story sacks include providing opportunities for children to:

- develop positive attitudes to books;
- become familiar with a core of books;
- listen to stories and other books;
- join in the retelling of a story;
- attend to and concentrate on books;
- develop their familiarity with the language of books;
- engage in conversations about books and reading;
- explore fiction and information books;
- learn about the uses of reading; and
- learn about how to read.

Curiosity kits

The success of story sacks has prompted others to think of similar resource banks that can be used to bring literacy alive for young children. Curiosity kits (Lewis and Fisher, 2003) are one such resource. These are book bags containing items such as:

- a non-fiction book;
- a commercial magazine on the same topic;
- toys or artefacts related to the topic;
- related print material such as an information leaflet or a newspaper article;
- suggestions for how to use the kit;
- suggestions for activities related to the topic; and
- a notebook for comments from home.

The magazine is intended to encourage adults at home to become involved with the kit and to provide children with a model of reading. The related print material shows children that print and reading are useful outside school and provide opportunities for children to see real applications of reading. The toys and artefacts give children the opportunity to explore the topic and reflect on or use their reading. The material in the curiosity kit can be linked to school projects, and some topics that have proved popular include space, dinosaurs, pets and sports. Curiosity kits have been particularly effective at encouraging boys to read and in involving male carers in reading with their children.

Story tapes

Story tapes and increasingly, CDs, of stories and rhymes can be placed in the listening area along with the appropriate books and story props. They give children another opportunity to listen to the book or practise reading with help from the tape. This boosts children's confidence, is enjoyable and contributes to their learning of story language and word recognition.

Class books

Practitioner-made enlarged texts are a valuable reading resource and add to the stock of materials in the class. During the course of a project, photographs can be taken of the children engaging in the different activities that have been planned. These can be mounted in a large home-made book and simple captions describing the activities can be written underneath the photographs. The finished book can be read to the class. Such books are very popular with the children as they like to read about themselves and their friends. The photographs and their familiarity with the activities that are depicted help the children to read the captions and have the opportunity to recognize some words.

It is also possible to create class versions of known story books in shared writing. These can be simplified retellings or they can feature children in the class. One class made a book about their headteacher entitled 'Where's Jacqui?' which was based on *Where's Spot?* (Hill, 1980). The words on each page asked questions similar to those in the original book such as 'Is she in her office?' and 'Is she in the playground?' The questions were composed by the class in shared writing and the children produced the illustrations. The repetition and the illustrations meant that this book could be read successfully by the children.

Making alphabets

Making alphabets for the classroom gives the children opportunities to learn about letters and sounds, and resources that the children make are more likely to be used by them than those that are just displayed. Many topics lend themselves to alphabets that will interest the children including food, television programmes and characters, toys, names and characters in books. The alphabets can be illustrated with photographs, pictures cut from magazines or catalogues, and food labels. The letters can be written by an adult or cut out from material that contains large print letters.

Reading area

The reading area is a standard part of every classroom. It should be freely available to the children and attractive and welcoming to them. It is an area where children can explore books, reread favourite books and share books with adults. It should contain:

- a variety of fiction, non-fiction and poetry books many of which will be books from the core book collection;
- single copies of books that have been used in guided reading;
- books made by children and teachers;
- comics and magazines;
- character toys that can support story reading;

■ story props related to some of the popular books; and

■ posters inviting children to read.

Conclusion

Beginning readers need to learn about reading as well as how to read. In this chapter I have tried to give examples of how practitioners can do both of these and so teach reading in meaningful and motivating ways.

Further reading

bfi education (2003) *Look Again!* London: British Film Institute.
This is a practical introduction to media literacy and how it can be planned for and taught in the early years.

Bromley, H. (2000) *Book-based Reading Games*. London: CLPE.
This practical book describes how to make book-based games to develop literacy and language.

Guppy, P. and Hughes. M. (1999) *The Development of Independent Reading*. Buckingham: Open University Press.
This is an excellent book that describes in detail the stages that children go through as they are learning to read. It suggests how adults can help children at each stage.

Tucker, N. (2002) *The Rough Guide to Children's Books 0–5*. London: Rough Guides/Penguin.
This is a helpful introduction to book selection for young children.

Chapter 4

Writing

Introduction

Writing is a complex activity which involves many skills. It includes deciding what one wants to write, how best to say it and how to put these ideas onto paper in a way that is intelligible to others. It takes time to become an accomplished writer and young children in the Foundation Stage are just beginning to acquire the understanding and abilities that they will need to become fluent writers. There is no need to rush this process; they have years ahead of them in which to learn. However, we can help children to make use of what they already know about writing, help them to understand the reasons for being able to write, and ensure that they enjoy the activity and develop their ability to write in age-appropriate ways. These should be the aims for practitioners in the Foundation Stage.

The uses of writing

In order to learn to write, children need to spend a great deal of time experimenting with and practising writing. If they are to give their time and attention to writing, they need to be convinced that it is a worthwhile and purposeful activity. They may have seen a range of writing types at home and in their community before they start in the nursery or reception class, but they may not fully understand the purposes of different sorts of writing or be aware of the relevance of writing to their own lives. Writing is a language form that is distinguished from speech because it can be permanent and it can be planned and changed before it emerges. Like talk it can be used to:

- entertain;
- persuade;

- express feelings;
- inform;
- request;
- instruct;
- record; and
- express opinions and ideas.

However, because it is a considered form of communication, it can fulfil these uses in a more sophisticated way than talk and, because it has a degree of permanence, the recipient of the writing does not need to be present while the message is created.

It is possible to help children to see different purposes for writing and its distinctive qualities through planning a varied writing curriculum, displaying different types of writing, and talking about writing. Using examples of different types of writing taken from texts that are familiar and interesting to young children illustrates that the different purposes for writing are relevant to them and can be used by them. Stories in books and comics, poems, rhymes and songs are examples of writing that is used to entertain. They have been written by authors who cannot be present but their words can be shared at any time. Advertisements for toys, sweets or food provide examples of writing that has been composed in order to persuade its audience to want or buy various products. They are written to make readers wish for what is being advertised and so have been composed very carefully. Greetings cards can be examined to show how feelings are expressed through writing and these are often sent to people who we do not see everyday. Notes and letters, perhaps those that are sent home to parents from school or specially written by the teacher, provide examples of requests or recounts. Shopping lists and till receipts show how writing can be used to provide a record. Captions and labels are found on information texts that are referred to frequently and so they need to have a degree of permanence.

In the Foundation Stage, children are expected to gain experience of a range of writing types and uses, including writing stories, poems and recounts and using writing to make lists, captions, instructions, signs, directions, menus, labels, greeting cards and letters (DfES, 2001a; QCA, 2000b). All these can be illustrated at school, often by real-life texts.

Aspects of writing

Writers have to do at least three things to produce a piece of writing. They have to:

- compose;
- transcribe; and
- review.

These are the three key elements in writing. Young children may have developed some awareness of these aspects of writing from watching or becoming involved in literacy events with adults or older children in the literate households and communities in which they live. This early understanding will be extended by adults during the children's time in the Foundation Stage.

Composition

Composing is about deciding what one wants to say and how one is going to say it. It is concerned with making decisions about the content of what is written and how to transmit the content in the most effective way. It also involves thinking about the audience or recipient of the writing by considering whether the writing will appeal to, and be accessible to, the reader. As children learn more about the purposes of writing and how to write, they will begin to use planning and drafting as part of the process of composition. Young children have ideas about what they want to write, and so can compose before they learn to spell or are adept at handwriting (Smith, 1982). In the nursery most writing will be spontaneous and convey a message that is immediate and linked to the context in which it is produced. In reception classes children will learn to take a more considered approach. They will be encouraged to think before they write, to use drawing as a way of planning their writing and to begin to structure their writing in ways that suit its purpose and audience.

Even very young children can tell stories and they gain more experience of how narrative is constructed from listening to stories and sharing books with adults. There is a good example of this in Chapter 7. Adults can extend children's awareness of how to compose by making a wide range of book-related resources available. These will include story props, puppets, dressing-up clothes, masks, role-play areas resourced to enable children to re-enact stories they have heard, and small-world toys. Discussions about characters, how stories begin and end and recalling the events in a story also provide opportunities for children to learn about composition.

Transcription

This refers to how writing is recorded, and includes spelling, handwriting, punctuation and presentation. In the *Curriculum Guidance for the Foundation*

Stage (QCA, 2000b) three of the Early Learning Goals refer specifically to transcription. In linking sounds and letters children learn about the relationship between letter sounds and letter shapes. This will help them to make use of phonic strategies when spelling simple, regular words and make plausible attempts at writing more complex words. Handwriting is an aspect of communication, language and literacy in its own right. By the end of the Foundation Stage children are expected to be able to manipulate writing implements comfortably and to be able to produce correctly formed letters. For punctuation children should be able to use some capital letters appropriately, for example at the start of their names, and they should be beginning to use full stops at the end of sentences.

Review

Reviewing what one has written involves rereading and appraising what has been written. It involves reading one's own work from the perspective of the reader and then making alterations to the content, style or presentation through editing or redrafting to make it more effective. This is a sophisticated skill that even many experienced writers do not fully master. However, the act of reflecting on writing and seeking ways to improve it can be fostered during the Foundation Stage. Teachers can model rereading and changing writing during shared writing. Children can engage in the process of reflection when adults read the writing that they produce, talk about it with them, write a correct version beneath the child's writing and write a comment or question that refers to the content of what has been written. This shared engagement and discussion about writing encourages children to think about what they have written and how they could improve their writing in the future.

How children learn to write

Studies of young children's literacy development suggest that children start to learn about writing and engage in writing behaviour before the age of 2 (Lancaster, 2003). Writing behaviour emerges when children have access to writing materials, see models of writing and observe people writing. In most areas of the developed world it is difficult for children to escape any of these. Print abounds not just in conventional ways such as in books and magazines, but also on clothing, toys, packaging, street signs and shop names. Children see adults write many things such as cheques, notes, greeting cards, lists and letters.

Very early writing may look like children's early drawings. Both may consist of dots, lines, curved shapes and shading. But by the age of 3 children are able to make the distinction between their intention to write and their intention to draw, and are able to say that one set of marks is a drawing and another set of marks is letters or writing (Harste et al., 1984). When talking about a drawing they have made they will talk about the dog or a dog, that is, they will use the definite or indefinite article in their description. If they are talking about their writing of the word *dog* they will omit the article and say this is dog or this says dog (Ferreiro and Teberosky, 1982). Talking about the illustration in Figure 4.1, Stephanie, aged 3, said *This is my mummy going shopping* and, pointing to the left of the picture, said, *This is the supermarket.* An over-zealous adult keen to see signs of writing in Stephanie's picture might have wanted to identify the circular shapes and some of the other marks as early letter shapes but Stephanie was clear that this was a picture not writing.

Figure 4.1 *Stephanie's drawing*

Clay (1975) suggested that once children can discriminate between drawing and writing their early mark-making reveals their developing knowledge about print. Children often use the same marks over and over, indicating their understanding that writing is about repeating a limited set of marks. They arrange their writing across the page and from top to bottom, showing their awareness of the directionality of writing in English. They use their stock of symbols to produce pieces of writing that say different things, showing that they realize that writing is generated from a limited number of symbols. Often children seem to be organizing their knowledge of symbols, letters and words as they produce lists of what they know. Children also explore the flexibility of writing, as they use the letters they know in order to make different letters by turning them round and writing them in different directions. Children who are experimenting with writing in these ways are learning about what counts as writing in English. This experimentation with a limited set of symbols can be seen in Avais's writing in Figure 4.2. Avais was using some of the letters in his name to write but he seems to be exploring the orientation of the *v* sometimes producing *z*- and *w*-like shapes.

Figure 4.2 *Avais's name*

In the very early stages of writing, children may not be able to tell an adult what their writing says. They may not yet understand that a writer creates the message. This is not always clear to children because as people write they are often silent and do not always read aloud what they have written. However, adults do read what other writers have written. They read books, street signs and letters that they have not composed. So while children may know that writing has a meaning that can be recovered, the models of writers that they have seen may lead them to believe that it is the reader who creates the message. Children may ask adults to read what their writing says or be content to explain to an adult that their writing is about something such their house or their holiday. Gradually children realize that they have the power to create the message and that they can read back what they have written. At this stage children may attribute quite long stories or descriptions to a fairly brief piece of writing consisting of a collection of apparently random symbols.

Once children understand that writing communicates a meaning and that it has a number of functions, they start to experiment with different types of writing. Labelling is very often one of the first kinds of writing that children use. They may label possessions and pictures with their name to denote ownership. They may use a more extended form of labelling by producing captions for their drawings such as, *This is my car*. Models for this kind of writing are often found in books specially written for young readers. In Figure 4.3 Annya, a 4-year-old in a nursery class, demonstrated her understanding of labelling in this piece of work produced in the writing area. The word *flower* is clearly written inside the drawing.

Other early forms of writing that are found in children's independent writing are recounts where children reconstruct personal experiences and events for others to read, procedural texts which tell others what to do such as *don't touch* or *keep out*, and records and notes such as lists or telephone messages. Some children may produce narratives, perhaps imitating the stories they have heard and enjoyed. Bashir, a 5-year-old pupil in a reception class produced the piece of writing in Figure 4.4 for a display about what children enjoyed about school. It reads, *I like swimming pool. Goggles. hat. I like coming to the school building.* The repetition of *I like* in his writing and the use of complete sentences in his writing may well be a reflection of books that have been read to him or that he has read.

Young children produce and experiment with a range of texts if they have experience of models of different types of writing and are given opportunities and encouragement to write in different ways. At school these opportunities can be situated in the imaginative play area, connected to

Figure 4.3 *Annya's flower*

other areas of the curriculum, prompted by the resources that are available in the writing area or suggested by the teacher.

Approaches to teaching writing

There are two main ways in which young children are taught to write in school. Briefly summarized, in the first, children tell an adult what they want to write, the adult writes this down and the child copies what the teacher has written. In the second, the child writes independently and then the adult responds to what the child has written.

Copying

The first method assumes that children's first encounters with writing take place when they start nursery or school and ignores any previous

Figure 4.4 *Bashir's writing*

experience that children may have had with writing. Children are taught to write by copying letters and words and memorizing letter sounds. For more extended writing children dictate a sentence to the adult who then writes this for the child to copy. Sometimes the sentence is written with a highlighter pen and the child traces over the adult version. This sort of writing is often linked to a picture that the child has drawn or to a piece of news that the child is asked to write. The adult sets the agenda for what is written and provides the model for children to copy. The children may engage in a limited amount of composition as they are asked to think of their own sentence, and their offering might be altered to make a complete sentence by the adult before it is written out for copying. There is little opportunity to review the writing, as the review will have taken place prior to writing when the adult helps the child to shape his or her thoughts into a sentence. The adult knows beforehand what the child has written and so will have little to say about the composition. As the child is copying, the spelling is also likely to be accurate. Consequently, the feedback from the adult is often about the neatness of the writing rather than what has been written. Comments might include phrases such as 'good try' or 'well done' rather than a genuine response to content. This method tends to place the emphasis on transcription or getting writing to look right as the child spends more time on copying or tracing than on discussing and shaping the content. There is little attention given to writing for an audience other than the teacher as it is unlikely that anyone other than the teacher will read the writing.

This approach to teaching young children to write encourages children to become dependent on the teacher and to learn that writing is so difficult that it is impossible to do it without adult help (Heenan, 1986). This may deter children from choosing to experiment with writing independently and from gaining extra practice at writing. It also teaches children that writing is mainly concerned with transcription, neat handwriting, correct spelling and meeting adult demands, rather than content and communication. In the long term such an approach may have a detrimental effect on children's composition as their dependency on adult help may prevent them from taking risks with their writing. Rather than making adventurous and interesting choices about words, they may limit what they say in their writing to words they know they can spell. If they do not understand the distinctive purposes of writing as a method of communication and recording, they may not see the point of writing and this may lead to a reluctance to write.

Developmental approaches

The second approach to teaching writing is when children are encouraged to write unaided. They are allowed to write what they want to in any way that they can, although teachers may suggest topics. They compose and transcribe by drawing on their own experience of observing writing and writers through living in literate households and a print-rich society, and of observing and participating in writing events in the classroom. At first the child's writing may bear little resemblance to conventional writing, but feedback from adults and greater experience with writing and written language through reading and writing activities give children the knowledge and understanding that they need in order to gradually refine what they write and how they write it. Their writing passes through the stages outlined in the previous section in this chapter, 'How children learn to write'. This approach has parallels with the early emergence of spoken language when the child's first utterances are accepted and responded to by adults who provide feedback and models that shape the child's emerging language until it becomes recognizable speech. Adults have a key role in helping children to learn to write in a developmental approach, as they build on what children know about writing and can do and extend this in ways that are relevant to individual learners.

In a developmental approach writing is seen as emerging as the child practises writing and receives support and feedback from adults. Such an approach acknowledges the continuity between early literacy behaviour and the behaviour of experienced writers. While accepting that children's early writing will not necessarily look like adults' writing, practitioners know that, with guidance and teaching, over time young children's writing will increasing resemble that of experienced writers. Developmental writing sits most easily within the child-initiated, practical and play-based method of organizing learning in the Foundation Stage as children are encouraged to actively engage in writing in contexts that are relevant to them. It also fits in with the suggestions about organizing for writing that is given in the *Curriculum Guidance for the Foundation Stage* (QCA, 2000b: 44) which says that in the Foundation Stage children need to be given opportunities 'to see adults writing and to experiment with writing for themselves through making marks, personal writing, symbols and conventional script'.

Developmental writing fits in with our understanding that young children learn through trying things out and getting feedback from adults that is appropriate to what they need to know. As I wrote in Chapter 1, young children learn through:

- active engagement and exploration;
- taking risks;
- collaboration with others;
- taking the initiative in learning;
- doing things that are relevant and enjoyable to them; and
- doing things that are important to them.

When children are learning in this way the adult's role in teaching children to write is to:

- give children time to explore, experiment, think and develop as writers;
- provide experiences and materials that stimulate children to write;
- provide children with models of how to write;
- provide opportunities for children to practise and apply their skills;
- provide answers to questions;
- provide explanations about social practices and activities;
- expect children to learn and acknowledge their learning;
- provide an environment in which it is safe to take risks; and
- respond to and provide for children in ways that are appropriate to their understanding and interests.

Gradually children's ability to produce readable writing increases as they produce writing, receive feedback, see writers at work, engage in reading and incorporate their understanding from these experiences into their repertoire of knowledge about writing.

Creating an environment for writing

In the Foundation Stage children need opportunities every day to learn about and experiment with writing. Adults need to create an environment that encourages children to write and to see writing as an enjoyable and productive activity.

Cambourne (1988) has suggested a number of classroom conditions that help children to learn to write and help to develop positive attitudes to writing. These conditions are:

- immersion;
- demonstration;
- expectations;
- responsibility;
- employment;
- approximation;
- response; and
- engagement.

If children are to learn to write they need to be surrounded by or immersed in print. They need to have access to books, notices, posters, songs, poems, children's writing, teacher-made books and charts and environmental print, and to have such print read to them and discussed with them. Teacher-made notices and labels can be written with the children so that children feel involved and know what the writing says. A print-rich environment provides children with models of the layout, symbols, types and uses of writing.

In order to be able to write independently children need to see how writers write. They need to see adults composing and talking about what they are doing and the decisions they are making as they translate their ideas into written symbols. Shared writing provides an ideal opportunity for teachers to demonstrate how to write. In shared writing adults can show children how to write and make explicit the thinking that underpins the production of a written text. They can vocalize how they select and alter what they are writing, how to use punctuation and the strategies they use to spell words, including sounding out, using analogy and making use of resources in the classroom and words in the environment.

Adults expect children to learn to talk; similarly adults need to expect that children will learn to write. We know from the studies of young children's emerging writing described in Lancaster (2003) that children are motivated to engage with writing from a very early age. Positive feedback that indicates that their efforts are valued and that begins to shape children's writing suggests to children that they can write and that writing is an important activity.

Children need to be given the opportunity to take some responsibility for their own learning. They need to be allowed to make choices about what and when they write. So, in addition to planned writing activities, other opportunities for writing need to be available. Children can be given responsibility for the spelling of what they write by expecting that they will use approximate spellings or make use of some of the spelling aids in the classroom. Adults need to accept the unaided and independent writing that children produce, identify what the child can do in writing, and acknowledge that children all know different things and will make progress at different rates.

In order to develop a skill, learners need to practise and use that skill regularly in a variety of contexts and for real purposes. Developing writers need to practise writing every day, for the teacher, a family member, a friend or an audience that has been created such as a character in a book or themselves. As they employ their skill and share their writing with others, they will receive feedback from the recipients that may help them to see what else they could do in their writing to make it clearer or more suited to its purpose, and this will guide and motivate them to find out how to develop their writing further.

In the early stages children's writing will only approximate to conventional writing. These early efforts need to be treated with respect by adults. Pointing out the errors or ignoring the importance of such attempts will give children negative messages about their ability to write. This may curtail children's willingness to have a go at writing and affect their confidence and enjoyment of writing. In order to learn to write, children need to write, to try out their hypotheses and make mistakes. Adults need to accept approximations in order that children continue to take risks and experiment with their writing.

The adult's role in developing writing is critical. Their response to children's writing will make a difference to their attitudes towards writing as well as their ability to write. Their initial response should be positive, informative and non-threatening. It should focus on the content and the meaning rather than the transcription. Adults may also make use of other aspects of classroom provision to foster further learning. Children could be encouraged to look at books and notices in the room. They could be provided with a demonstration of writing through written feedback on the piece of writing or through shared writing. They could be encouraged to try out another similar or connected piece of writing and so gain more practice.

The effectiveness of these seven aspects of classroom provision are all dependent on engagement. Children have to actively participate in writing and regard writing as an important and purposeful activity if they are to make progress as writers. Sometimes children do not engage with writing because they do not understand its uses. They may find it difficult or too risky. Adults need to show children that writing has many distinct and important uses and to make learning to write as comfortable as possible. If children do not see writing as something that they want to do, their learning from classroom resources, demonstrations, practice and feedback will be limited. Children who are interested in writing will make more use of the opportunities and experiences that are offered to them.

Teaching writing

Shared writing

Shared writing is a technique that can be used with the whole class, large groups or small groups of children. It is a powerful tool for demonstrating and developing the compositional skills of writing. It can also help children to understand the transcriptional elements of writing as they see how letters and words are formed and arranged on the page. It enables all children to participate in and learn about writing without having to write themselves. This is very helpful for inexperienced writers who may struggle with transcription. There are three different ways of doing shared writing (DfEE, 2001):

- teacher demonstration;
- teacher scribing and;
- supported composition.

The first two of these have a firm place in the Foundation Stage. Supported composition makes more demands on children's ability to write and so may be helpful towards the end of the reception year.

In teacher demonstration the children watch and listen as the practitioner models how the text is composed. The adult thinks aloud as the text is written, rehearsing the sentence before writing, making changes to the construction or to words and explaining why the changes are being made. In this way the thinking that goes on during composition is being modelled by the teacher. The practitioner can also draw attention to the place on the flip chart or interactive whiteboard where the writing begins and how it is written across and then down the page. As the words are written the adult can enunciate them clearly in order to draw attention to the links between the sounds of words and the way they are written.

In teacher scribing the practitioner writes as the children contribute. The adult may challenge the children's contributions in order to refine their thinking and their compositional skills. The children may be asked to discuss their contributions with a talk partner before making suggestions about what should be included. The practitioner may comment on the suitability of the suggestions or ask the children to do so. This discussion about what should be included provides a model for children of how to review writing.

Supported composition normally takes place within a teacher scribing session. Alone or in pairs children write parts of the text on dry wipe boards or in notebooks. This is more inclusive than asking one child to write on the class flip chart. In order to make teaching points, successful examples are commented on and misconceptions are discussed before one of the children's suggestions is scribed by the teacher on a whiteboard or flip chart. In the reception class this could be done with a group of children as a guided writing activity.

In the Foundation Stage shared writing can be used to:

- record shared events;
- provide reminders of future events;
- label classroom equipment;
- write notices;
- demonstrate the types of writing that the children may try out in the role-play area;
- demonstrate the types of writing that children may try out in the writing area;
- list words that the children may want to write; and
- prepare for a writing activity that the children will attempt later.

Guided writing

This gives children the opportunity to write independently but with support. For young children in the reception class, guided writing sessions may initially focus on the production of a short piece of text and may be combined with a craft or art activity such as making and writing a greeting card or making a story map with an adult. Short pieces of text that can be written in guided writing could include making captions for use in class, making written signs and other resources for the imaginative play area. As the reception year progresses teachers may want to use guided writing to give children the opportunity to write the types of texts that have been demonstrated in shared writing. The adult who is leading the activity will remind the children about how to write this particular type of text and ask the children to think about what they are going to write before they begin. As they write the adult can discuss the content and structure of what is written. Guided writing can also be used to introduce children to planning, for example, how to construct and use a storyboard, or it can be used to demonstrate how to review and develop ideas in writing. Guided writing gives the teacher the opportunity to observe and monitor the strategies that children are using as they write, as well as their involvement and confidence as writers. This information can be acted upon in individual conferences or in devising tasks that suit children's stage of development.

Sometimes in guided writing in the Foundation Stage the adult may scribe for the group of children, thus enabling them to gain experience in extended composition. These texts could be used later as reading material or the children could read onto a tape what has been written. The texts and the tapes can be shared with the whole class and then become a permanent resource in the class.

Independent writing

Independent writing gives the children the opportunity to have a go at writing by themselves. In the nursery, independent writing will often arise as part of children's play or in the writing area. In reception there will be additional set times each week for children to write. Some independent writing will probably be closely linked to the shared writing that the teacher has modelled.

Giving feedback

Giving feedback is a powerful method of teaching writing. Children deserve a genuine response to their efforts and they need a response if their ability to write is to develop. They need the advice of a knowledgeable adult to help them to fill in the gaps in their own knowledge. Such advice has to be given sensitively. If children receive too much advice they will be overwhelmed and unable to use it. They may feel that what they have done is of little value. If it is at a level that is inappropriate children may feel that writing is too hard for them. The practitioner's suggestions need to be carefully selected, informative and non-threatening. The feedback might involve a demonstration of how to do something. It might involve a written response to what has been written in order to show that the content of the writing is valued and to give the child a personal demonstration of writing. It might involve telling the child about a resource that they could use to help them when they are writing. Whatever the response it should be tailored to the child's needs.

Activity

Look at the writing in Figure 4.4. After congratulating Bashir on his work, how would you respond to this piece of writing? Would you:

Ask him to reread his first sentence in order to help him spot the missing *the* and to encourage habits of rereading and self correction?
Write a question for him to respond to such as, *Can you swim yet?* in order to prompt him to write a little more and provide him with a correct version of the word *swim*?
Write a response that focuses on the content of what he wrote for example, *I like going to the swimming pool, too,* in order to show him that the messages in writing are important and are responded to by readers, to illustrate the correct spelling of *like* and *swimming pool* and to show him the lower case letter formation needed in the words in this sentence?
Or would you respond in some other way?

Activity

Look at the writing in Figure 4.5. This was produced by 3-year-old Andrew. How would you initiate a conversation with Andrew to find out what he intended to say through his writing? How would you comment on his efforts?

Figure 4.5 *Andrew's writing*

For information, when Andrew showed his writing to the practitioner he said, 'I am good at writing my name.'

The literacy hour in the Foundation Stage

Although the literacy hour as an hour dedicated to developing reading and writing does not need to be introduced until the third term of the reception year, a number of elements and teaching strategies are appropriate for children throughout the Foundation Stage. Shared writing can be introduced to children in the nursery as it enables them to participate in writing activities even though they might find independent writing difficult. Activities to develop phonemic awareness and phonic knowledge which help with spelling can be a part of most nursery sessions. Guided writing should be introduced in the reception year and should be planned for each child each week from the start.

Writing activities and resources

For nursery age children the most suitable activities are those with a limited amount of writing, where children explore stories orally and through play, where children can experiment with writing independently or where adults scribe for children. Children in reception classes continue to benefit from these practices but, in addition, there will be more planned writing activities linked to a topic or a book that has been shared with the class. Through shared reading and shared writing children will be introduced to different types of writing and be expected to use a range of writing formats.

Imaginative play area

Play offers children opportunities to:

- learn about the tools, materials and activities associated with literacy;
- develop and refine their capacity to use symbols, to represent experience and to construct imaginary worlds; and
- make the roles and activities of people who read and write more meaningful and accessible.

Imaginative play areas give children the opportunity to see the uses of writing and use writing in a variety of ways, as well as allowing them to explore and gain practice at writing. In order for children to get the most out of an imaginative play area that has been resourced for literacy, adults need to play alongside children modelling the sort of writing that can occur there. The area should be freely available for the children to use and may be timetabled as one of the activities for the literacy hour in reception classes.

Imaginative play areas can be realistic or imaginary. Realistic play areas help to make links between children's experiences of writing in their communities and their experiences of writing in school. They show children real-life purposes for writing. Examples of realistic play areas might include a cinema or a corner shop. There are now many videos and digital versatile discs (DVDs) of children's books available, and some of these could be available in the cinema. It would be particularly fitting if the videos that were shown related to a book that was being shared with the class or the video itself could be used as a stimulus for language and literacy activities as described in Chapter 3. In the cinema the children could make and write tickets, posters, programmes, labels, prices and receipts for sweets, popcorn, ice cream and soft drinks. A corner shop, perhaps also containing a post office, offers a range of activities for language and literacy. It could contain comics, newspapers, greetings cards, foodstuffs, sweets, snacks, maps, newspapers, toys, stamps, envelopes, writing paper and forms. The children could make video covers, posters, receipts and write letters and cards to be posted. Imaginative play areas can also be established outdoors. In the summer there could be a garden centre where the children could write labels, posters, flyers, receipts and at the end of the project hold a sale which would include making special offer notices. If the imaginative play area is linked to a book it might be necessary to think creatively about the literacy resources that are included, as few books show characters involved in writing. Asking the children about the sort of literacy activities that they think characters might carry out can be a productive speaking and listening activity as well as making them aware of the writing activities that they can carry out in the play area. For example asking children about the literacy materials that the Three Bears and Goldilocks might use could result in the following:

- newspapers and magazines for Daddy and Mummy Bear;
- recipe books, particularly for porridge;
- picture books for Baby Bear;
- shopping lists; and
- letters and cards for special events and to and from Goldilocks.

These materials could then be placed inside the Three Bears' house.

Writing area

Most nursery and reception classes have an area of the classroom dedicated to writing. This is a place which children can choose to use or adults can suggest that they use it if children express an interest in writing. Its use can also be planned as part of literacy sessions. Children often use the area to repeat a writing activity that has been demonstrated to them, such as making get well cards for dolls and soft toys if they have previously made a get well card for a character such as Humpty Dumpty. They can sometimes make resources for their play, such as a register if they are playing at school. Some children like to write a note or a letter to take home or to give to the teacher.

Adults need to help children to use the area productively and to keep it fresh and stimulating. To do this they can join children as they use it and do some writing of their own to provide a model for the children. They can also suggest types of writing and people to write to, and they can change the resources. For example, at appropriate points in the year the area can be dedicated to making greetings cards. From time to time the area can contain a postbox where children can post notes and letters that they have written for members of the class. These can be delivered and read at the end of the day. The teacher could introduce a letter from the wolf in *Suddenly!* (McNaughton, 1996) asking for the children's help in catching Preston Pig. The children could be invited to write back with suggestions. Once some replies have been received the teacher, acting as the wolf, could write back to let the children know if their suggestions have been successful. This or similar activities can continue for a few days.

The area needs to be well resourced and inviting. It should contain a variety of writing implements and materials such as coloured paper, cards, booklets, postcards, envelopes and forms. There can also be a stapler, hole punch, paper clips, glue, scissors, guide lines, a whiteboard, plastic letters, alphabet books, picture dictionaries, in fact anything that adults or children might need to use when they are writing. A display board where children can pin their writing and where examples of writing and suggestions for topics are displayed is also useful.

Story maps

Many stories take the form of a journey for example, *Rosie's Walk* (Hutchins, 1970), *Hairy Maclary from Donaldson's Dairy* (Dodd, 1985) and *Once upon a time* (Prater, 1993). Such stories can be represented by a large map that can be drawn and labelled by the children working with an adult. In order to make the map and represent the scenes, events and characters that occur or are met on the journey, the children need to return to the book to check what happens and in what order. Drawing the items gives children the chance to become familiar with story structures, which is important if children are to produce well-written stories of their own. Once finished, models of houses, trees and other key elements or small-world toys can be added. The children can then play with the map, using it to retell the original story and then creating their own versions. Making and playing with story maps can prepare children for writing their own stories and is a way of introducing young children to planning and thinking about what they want to say before they begin to write.

Displays

Children can contribute to displays by writing captions, speech bubbles and labels. These may be accompanied by the teacher's writing. They can also make labels for their models. Some of the labels can be written in shared or guided writing sessions.

Sequencing

Sets of photographs or pictures can be used as a stimulus for writing. A group of photographs showing children engaged in the different stages of cooking can be ordered and then a caption can be written for each picture. Alternatively the photographs could be used as a prompt to write a set of instructions as in a recipe.

Pictures

All sorts of pictures and photographs can be used as a starting point for writing. The children can use their own individual photographs to write about themselves, their appearance, their likes or their dislikes. Pictures such as those of a park or a farm can provide a backdrop against which a short episode can be constructed. The children could cut out a character from a comic and move them around the picture, exploring the different parts of the park and the farm, and in doing so think about settings. Using the picture to tell the story orally allows children to plan what they might write. Children can also label pictures rather than attempting to write complete sentences. This gives them the opportunity to engage in writing non-fiction.

Construction

When work is planned around a book, teachers often devise model-making or construction tasks. These can lead the children into exploring a book further and so contribute to children's reading abilities and their understanding of a book. The models that are made can also be a starting point for writing. If children make the six houses in Aristotle Street as part of the work related to *Six Dinner Sid* (Moore, 1990) they could also make street signs and other street furniture which includes writing. Making a new bed and chair for Baby Bear after listening to *Goldilocks and the Three Bears* could be stimulus for writing captions for the models, a set of instructions about how to make the bed or chair, or an explanation of how the children made the furniture. These pieces of writing could be displayed next to the completed models along with the children's names.

Story boxes

A story box (Bromley, 2003) is a box containing items that can be used to create a story. They can help children learn about composition, planning and story language. The box is filled with small toys and objects based on a theme or a well-known story perhaps from the core book collection or familiar from the television. Examples might include contents related to *Old Bear* (Hissey, 1994), *Postman Pat, The Three Billy Goats Gruff* or *Where's Spot?* (Hill, 1980). The interiors of the boxes can be decorated to reflect the contents and so form a stage on which the characters can be placed. Using the characters and objects in the boxes, the children can tell stories that they compose. With modelling and experience the children will use story language as they compose, including words such as *Once upon a time, and then, at last* and repeated phrases and refrains. They are often used by pairs of children working together after their use has been modelled by the teacher. An adult might also work with the children to help them develop their story. The stories can be scribed by the teacher as a shared writing activity with the children, or older reception children might be able to write the stories for themselves. If written up by an adult the stories can be made into a class book for shared reading incorporating illustrations or photographs produced by the children. They can also be a stimulus for a guided writing session. Alternatively, the children could tell their story to the class during large-group time or during the plenary session in the literacy hour. Story boxes are helpful for bilingual learners or those with special educational needs, as their visual, three-dimensional nature provides children with tangible and practical references.

Sand and water play

Both the sand and water trays can be resourced to give children practice at retelling familiar stories and creating their own stories. Any story that is set in a desert or on the beach can be located in the sand tray. Examples might include, *Handa's Surprise* (Browne, 1994), *The Hunter* (Geraghty, 1994) or *Maisy at the Beach* (Cousins, 2002). Some of Shirley Hughes's poems from *Out and About throughout the Year* (2005) could also be set in the sand tray and this would give young children the chance to explore poetry and rhymes.

Many stories are set near rivers or the sea and the water tray is an ideal resource for allowing children to explore these stories in more detail. These might include *Mr Gumpy's Outing* (Burningham, 1978), *Who Sank the Boat?* (Allen, 1982) and *The Rainbow Fish* (Pfister, 1996). Like many of the activities suggested in this section, play in the sand and water trays can help children become familiar with story structure, characterization and setting. It can help children learn to compose and help them rehearse their own oral stories that can be written down by themselves or scribed by the teacher.

Storyboards

On storyboards children draw a series of pictures depicting the beginning, middle and end of a story plus one or more events from the story. These are drawn as a sequence. The number of pictures can be varied according to the age and writing ability of the children. Children can be encouraged to write a caption or sentence for each picture. The set of sentences should tell the story. More experienced children can be encouraged to incorporate story language into their writing. It is often helpful for the children to begin using a storyboard to retell a familiar published story and then to create a new version of a known story before writing their own stories. Storyboards introduce children to the idea of planning what they are going to write. They enable children to mentally compose each sentence as they draw and by drawing a sequence of pictures they are thinking about structure including openings and endings. In the reception class the drawing and writing of a storyboard can be spread over two or more literacy sessions. During the final session children can review their story and make changes to improve it if necessary.

Media texts

In Chapter 3 I suggested that videos, films, television programmes and advertisements could be used for shared reading. If used in this way they can also be used as a starting point for writing activities. Children know a great deal about the characters who appear in television programmes that they watch, and this knowledge can be used to explore characterization further. For example, watching videos and reading and discussing comics about the Tweenies could lead to a number of writing activities that depend for their success on the children's understanding of the characters. The children could be asked to:

- make a present and a greetings card for one of the Tweenies;
- make a dictionary of information about the Tweenies;
- write a letter or an e-mail to one of the Tweenies;
- research *The Tweenies* using the BBC website (www.bbc.co.uk/cbeebies/tweenies);
- design a menu for a Tweenies' café or design a menu for a Tweenies' picnic;
- design a poster using the computer advertising the Tweenies;
- make a Tweenies board game; or
- write a review of *The Tweenies*.

Building in opportunities to use ICT to research and write is particularly appropriate to today's 3-, 4- and 5-year-olds, as many of them are already competent users of technology and in 10 years' time the keyboard will be at least as important for writing as the pen, if not more so.

Taking time to teach writing

Some writing that is produced in nursery and reception classes may be a one-off. But some writing at the reception stage should be planned, written and reviewed. The following illustration of a sequence of writing sessions designed to introduce young children to writing a recount shows how this is possible.

The children have been on a visit to the local park where they had a picnic and played games. After the visit the children are going to write a postcard to take home to their parents to tell them about the outing. To create a recount the children need to include:

- where they went;
- when;
- why;
- what they did;
- who with; and
- some concluding remarks.

The day after the visit, during shared writing, the children and the teacher could create a bank of words related to the outing that the children might use later in the week in their independent writing. Such words might include *park, friends, picnic, played*. These could be read through and displayed in a prominent position in the room. Together in shared writing the teacher and children might compose the first sentence of the recount; for example, *On Monday I went to the park*. The children could copy this into the first section of a prepared storyboard. To follow this up the children could use story boxes, small-world play and construction toys to re-create the events of the visit to prepare them for their own writing on the following days. Some children, working with an adult might make story maps of the outing.

The next day the children could be asked to write two sentences on their storyboards recalling two things they did in the park. The children's ideas could be discussed and words they might need in their writing could be found on the word bank. Some children could be asked to extend their sentences from a basic *I played football* to *I played football with Henry and Jane*. The children could begin to draw a picture depicting one of the events that they had written about on one side of their postcard. On the next day the children and the teacher could discuss how to begin and end a message on a postcard. *Dear Mum, Dear Dad, Dear Nan* might be written on the flip chart. For the endings they might want to say what they enjoyed and why. The children could then start to write their postcards beginning with the salutation and then copying the writing from their storyboard. They could be asked to think of their own ending as they wrote or finished their illustrations and then put this directly onto the card. An adult might want to work with one group of children to help them draft their endings.

On the final day the children could write the name and address of the person they were giving the card to and finish any outstanding writing or drawing. During the composition of this recount, good examples of sentences could be shared with the class and the children could also be shown how to develop their writing to make it more interesting for the reader. Taking a number of days to produce a piece of writing helps children to understand how to write in a particular way, in this case: how to write a recount, to go through all the stages involved in writing, including planning, composition, review and revision, and to regard writing as a thoughtful and important activity.

How children learn to spell

Richard Gentry (1982) outlined a five-stage model of spelling development in English which shows how children's spelling develops from the pre-communicative when it is almost impossible to read what a child has written, to the conventional when most words are spelled correctly.

At the pre-communicative stage children use letter symbols and sometimes numerals to represent words. Upper and lower case letters may be used and the letters may be written from right to left or left to right. There is no correspondence between the letters that are written and the letters that would appear in the correct spelling of the word. The choice of letters seems random. In Figure 4.6, 4-year-old Peter's efforts to write his name show that he is at this stage of spelling.

Figure 4.6 *Peter's name*

The second stage is the semi-phonetic. This signals the child's first attempts to use letter sound correspondences in order to spell words. They may use letter names as well as letter sounds to denote what they hear. Generally children represent some of the consonants in the word but often omit the vowel sounds, producing spellings such as *ct* for *cat*. Words may be abbreviated and one letter may represent a whole word as in *T* for *tea*. At this stage writing is usually set out from left to right and words may be separated.

The next stage, the phonetic stage, shows how children begin to use their knowledge of the sound system of the language in a much more systematic way. The majority or all the sounds present in the word are represented in some way but this may still lead to some unconventional spellings such as *pApr* for *paper* or *nIt* for *night*. The child is concentrating on representing sounds rather than using the visual elements of spelling which will provide information about acceptable letter sequences. Words are separated by spaces. Although children's learning progresses at different rates, this is the stage that many children will have reached when they leave the Foundation Stage. They should be able to 'use their phonic knowledge to write simple regular words and make phonetically plausible attempts at more complex words' (QCA, 2000b: 60). Of course, some 5-year-old children may still be at one of the earlier stages. Edith's writing in Figure 4.7 is typical of many children in reception classes. She can spell simple phonically regular and frequently-used words correctly but uses a semi-phonetic strategy when trying to write *beautiful*, which is a long and difficult word.

Figure 4.7 *Edith's writing*

Some children at the end of the Foundation Stage may be moving gradually towards the next spelling stage, the transitional stage. Here children start to incorporate visual spelling strategies into their writing, resulting in some phonetic and some conventional spelling. They may be able to spell some words such as *you* and *the* from memory. Their understanding that there are different ways of representing sounds in English is growing. In order to spell unknown words they may make analogies with familiar letter patterns, producing words such as *nite* for *night* where they are drawing on their knowledge of the *ite* letter string. This stage may last for some time, until beyond the end of Key Stage 1.

In order to reach the final or conventional spelling stage, children need to know about word structure, including connections between words such as *medical* and *medicine*, prefixes, suffixes, compound words and silent and double consonants. At this stage they have a good knowledge of word structure and they can visualize words and judge whether their spelling looks right. Knowledge about how to spell is firmly established, even if every word is not spelled correctly. The aim is for children to reach this stage by about the age of 11.

Teaching spelling

In order for children to learn about spelling and for teachers to teach, it is essential that children are given opportunities to write independently. As Smith (1982: 187) wrote, 'Learning to spell takes time; it begins with misspelling.' It is impossible to assess children's spelling development or the strategies they are using if children's writing is always copied. It is only possible to teach if we know what children can do and where they need help.

For most children their earliest spelling strategy is a phonetic one. To use this strategy they need to analyse the sounds they hear in words and work out how to represent them. Developing an awareness of the sounds that can be heard in words is the key to developing semi-phonetic and phonetic strategies. To help children use phonetic strategies it is helpful to begin by, first, developing children's phonological awareness and, then, developing their phonemic awareness.

Phonological awareness is an awareness of the sounds of the language and it encompasses an ability to identify and catagorize the sounds that are heard in words. Goswami (1999) has suggested that there are three stages of phonological awareness associated with hearing sounds in words. The first is an awareness of and ability to segment words into syllables. The second is an awareness of onset, the part of the syllable before the first vowel, and rime, the part of the syllable from the first vowel onwards. The third stage is an awareness of phonemes or the smallest unit of sounds in words. These three aspects of phonological awareness are illustrated in Figure 4.8.

Learning about syllables through drawing attention to the rhythm of words and language helps children to listen to and recognize the sounds of individual words. This understanding of syllabification continues to play an important part in spelling beyond the early stages, as it helps writers to segment multisyllable words into manageable spelling units. Once children can recognize syllables, learning to split individual syllables into onsets and rimes helps them to analyse the sounds in words in more detail. Becoming aware of onsets leads directly into learning about initial phonemes, as many onsets are single sounds. Knowing about rimes is very beneficial in helping children to sort out how to write medial vowel sounds, which can be a problem for young writers at the semi-phonetic stage as looking at rimes draws attention to the vowels that occur inside words. Rimes also help children to make connections between words. For example, Jack's understanding of the onsets and rimes in his name should help him to spell *back*, *lack*, *pack* and *sack* if he is shown how to make analogies or connections between words. This ability to make connections between the words they know and words with the same rime is important and helpful to young spellers. It helps them to draw on their memory of letter patterns in known words in order to write unfamiliar words.

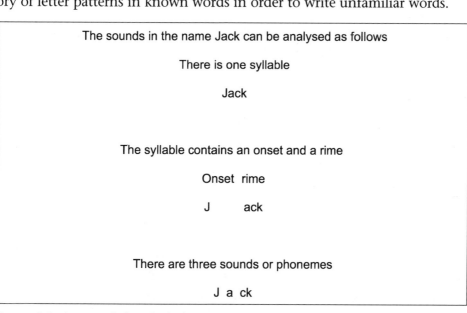

Figure 4.8 *Aspects of phonological awareness*

Syllabification, onset and rime, awareness of phonemes and making analogies are the aspects of spelling that children are introduced to in the Foundation Stage. In addition, they should be encouraged to develop visual strategies as these are essential if children are to become independent spellers. Looking carefully at words and making collections of words that share the same onsets and collections of words containing the same rimes begins this process of developing visual strategies. This is especially the case if the collections are displayed and used for sorting and matching activities.

Activities to develop spelling

In order to learn how to spell, children need the opportunity to learn about grapho-phonemic relationships through demonstration, games and activities, and they need opportunities to produce their own writing and receive feedback on what they have written, engage in discussions about their words and see models of correct spelling. Some specific activities are listed below.

Syllabification

- Clap out the rhythms in nursery rhymes, poems and songs.
- Clap out the rhythms and syllables in the children's names, food items and toys.
- During shared reading and writing select a word and clap out the syllables.
- Make up new verses to poems and nursery rhymes maintaining the same rhythm as the original.

Onset and rime

- Sing songs and say poems together to foster awareness of rhyme.
- Read stories that contain strong rhyming patterns such as *The Green Queen* (Sharratt, 1992).
- Use words from rhyming texts to look at onsets and rimes.
- Play I spy as a rhyming game, looking for something that rhymes with the original word.
- Play odd one out using two rhyming and one non-rhyming word.
- Sort pictures of objects according to their rimes.
- Provide children with cards, some with onsets and some with rimes, and challenge the children to make up recognizable words.
- Incorporate common rimes into handwriting practice.

Analogy

- Make collections of words that share the same rimes.
- Use magnetic letters to make words and to change the onset to make new words.
- Use shared writing of songs and nursery rhymes to experiment with changing words.
- Demonstrate how to attempt unfamiliar words during shared writing.

- Use whiteboards to ask children to write down words that share the same rime as the target word.

Phonemic awareness

- Make letter shapes using clay and play dough.
- Make alphabet books and friezes based on children's names, animals, television characters.
- Sing alphabet songs and rhymes.
- Play alphabet games such as I went to market.
- Involve children in helping to spell words during shared writing.
- Encourage children who are writing random symbols to write down what they can hear.
- Match initial letters to a collection of objects.
- Make personal alphabet books in which they stick pictures of items that begin with the appropriate letter.

Visual awareness

- Make children's names using modelling clay, paint and magnetic letters.
- Sort and compare collections of children's names and the names of characters from books.
- Play games that use key words from familiar books.
- Create a class dictionary of words that children write frequently.
- Play lotto, pairs and snap using a limited number of key words.
- Demonstrate correct spelling and word boundaries by writing beneath children's writing.
- Scribe for individual children to provide them with models of correct spelling.
- Work on spellings of words that the child can almost spell correctly.

Handwriting

Handwriting is a system that follows a number of rules. In English writing is arranged left to right across the page and top to bottom down the page. Each letter has definite start and exit points, and needs to be made in a particular way. Letters also have specific heights. Some letters are very similar as they are mirror images of each other and this can be confusing for young children. Upper and lower case letters have different forms and are used differently. Spaces as well as symbols are important in handwriting, as they are used to mark word boundaries and letter boundaries. These rules need to be learned by children if they are to develop a readable and fluent style of handwriting.

Teaching handwriting

If children are given access to resources and models of writing, and are encouraged to write, their handwriting passes through a number of stages. At first they produce straight vertical and horizontal lines, often gripping their pencil very hard and holding it in their fist. They progress to producing curved or scribble-like shapes which gradually extend across the page and resemble adult cursive script. Gradually children include some recognizable letter-like shapes into their writing. These may be upper and lower case forms. They may repeat the same letter shape over and over. The letters that they include in their writing may be those that occur in their names. Gradually, they include more letters into their writing and begin to leave spaces to mark boundaries between words. If children are left to their own devices, the letter shapes that they produce are rarely correctly formed. Children need active teaching, direct intervention and opportunities to practise making letter shapes in the correct way. As Sassoon (2003) suggests, handwriting is a taught skill as a fluent, comfortable and readable script in which letters can be joined easily does not emerge naturally.

In the Foundation Stage children may not have established a dominant hand for writing and manipulating tools. They will need to be allowed to pick up writing implements with whatever hand they prefer in order to allow them to discover their preferred hand. About 10 per cent of the population is left-handed and left-handers find writing from left to right more difficult than right-handers, so adults need to consider their needs when teaching handwriting. Practitioners should model letter formation with their left hand for those children who are left-handed. It helps if left-handed writers tilt their paper slightly to the right as this helps them to see what they have written. They are also helped if their fingers are about 1 to 2 centimetres away from the end of the writing implement.

In order to reach the Early Learning Goal for writing, which involves being able to form most letters correctly, children need to develop a number of skills including:

- good gross and fine motor control;
- a recognition of pattern;
- a language to talk about shapes and movements; and
- the main handwriting movements involved in the three basic letter shapes as exemplified by l, c and r (DfEE, 2001: 157).

Gross motor control

Physical development activities such as games, cycling, climbing and dance will all help children to gain increasing control of their bodies and contribute towards developing more delicate motor control, strength and balance. Activities which will help include:

- encouraging children to make large movements in the air with their arms;
- making shapes that resemble letter shapes using the whole body and parts of the body;
- drawing large letter shapes in the air; and
- painting large letter shapes.

Pattern

Patterns need to contribute towards children's ability to make the four basic strokes and shapes that are used to produce most letters. Vertical lines that start at the top are used to form i, j, l, t and u; arch-like shapes which start at the top, go down and retrace upwards are used in b, h, m, n, p and r; round shapes that move in an anti-clockwise direction are used in c, a, d, e, g, o, q, f and s; and diagonal lines are used in k, v, w, x, y and z. Patterns should be made from left to right across the page to encourage children to internalize the left to right direction of writing in English. Children can make patterns in paint, with felt tips, pencils and wax crayons. The resulting patterns can be displayed as art works in their own right. Patterns can also be made to frame pieces of writing or pictures and large strips of paper on which children have made patterns can be used to surround classroom displays.

The vocabulary of handwriting

Describing the movements that are made when writing letters helps children to establish the movements that they need to make to form letters in the correct way. It encourages them to use the right shapes and to move in the right direction. It also helps if adults and children have a shared language to discuss letter shapes.

Fine motor control

This gives children control over writing implements. Activities which strengthen children's finger and hand muscles and give them experience of manipulating a range of tools all help to develop fine motor control. Practical activities taken from the curriculum for creative development will all contribute to refining motor control. Specific activities which help include:

- those which include cutting and sticking;
- sewing and weaving activities;
- chopping and peeling in cooking activities;
- modelling using clay, play dough and modelling clay;
- using different sized paintbrushes for painting; and
- construction activities.

Letter formation

This can be practised by:

- making letter jigsaws;
- making letter shapes on each other's backs;
- tracing letter shapes in damp sand, cornflour and rice;
- painting; and
- making patterns involving letters.

Punctuation

By the end of the Foundation Stage children are expected to 'begin to form simple sentences, sometimes using punctuation' (QCA, 2000b: 64) and 'use a capital letter for the start of their own name' (DfES, 2001a: 18). There are limited expectations for how much use young children can make of punctuation, as the correct use of punctuation is a difficult skill and one which develops slowly.

Young children can become fascinated with punctuation marks. In particular they seem to enjoy reproducing exclamation marks once they have seen them in books. This interest in punctuation is important and should be encouraged, but it does not mean that children understand why and when exclamation marks are used. Some children also like using full stops and may intersperse their writing with large dots between words or end every line of their writing with a full stop. Again this interest in punctuation is a sign that children are becoming aware of more and more features of writing but it will take some time before they are able to use full stops correctly.

The correct use of a full stop depends on understanding its function. Children need to understand the concept of a sentence, something which is very difficult to define (Smith, 1982). However at a simple level a sentence contains an idea and after marking a sentence the writer moves on to expand on the idea or begins to write about a new idea in the next sentence. A sentence also needs to be meaningful and to be complete in the sense that it contains a verb and probably a subject and an object. There is a great deal to know about in order to make decisions about where to place full stops and children need to recognize the purpose of punctuation in order to use it correctly. The need for full stops only becomes clear when children produce extended pieces of writing and they need to identify the different ideas in their writing. Hall (1999) suggests that children probably benefit from some explicit instruction and explanation about punctuation in order to learn about it. In addition, and before any teaching is useful, children need opportunities to experience and explore punctuation and to receive feedback. This is particularly true in the early years.

In Figure 4.4 Bashir seems to be exploring the use of punctuation in his writing. He has used full stops to demarcate the items in the list of things he needs for swimming. This might indicate that he is ready to think about the correct use of full stops and this could be discussed with him and demonstrated on this piece of writing, which contains two complete sentences. Contextualizing teaching about punctuation by using the children's own work is the most helpful way of introducing children to its use. If skills are taught out of context they rarely transfer to everyday work.

Conclusion

Children learn about writing most easily when literacy activities are embedded in daily classroom activities or a context that is relevant to them. They become interested in writing when it has a purpose that they can understand. They need frequent, varied, relevant and authentic opportunities to write. Staff in the Foundation Stage need to value writing and to create an ethos that leads children to think that they are joining a community in which writing is enjoyed, needed and valued.

Further reading

O'Sullivan, O. and Thomas, A. (2000) *Understanding Spelling*. London: CLPE.
This book is a practical yet scholarly examination of learning to spell and teaching children to spell. Although it covers the whole primary age

range, the chapters describing the authors' research and their findings are helpful to teachers in the Foundation Stage and there are specific sections on the teaching of spelling in reception classes.

Whitehead, M. (2002) *Developing Language and Literacy with Young Children*. 2nd edn. London: Paul Chapman Publishing.
This book is worth reading from cover to cover. It includes all aspects of language and literacy, and has a very helpful chapter on writing development.

Chapter 5

Inclusion

Introduction

Inclusion means that all children have the right to have their learning needs met. It refers not just to children who have special needs but also to those who are gifted and talented or who may in the past have been discriminated against, such as children from traveller families or those who are looked after by the local authority. Schools and settings are expected to make any adaptations necessary to cater for the needs of all children.

In this Chapter I consider how early years settings can offer inclusive education and consider this in relation to children with special educational needs (SEN) related to communication, language and literacy. Some of the issues discussed in this chapter have been introduced in other chapters in this book, but this separate chapter allows some of the issues and procedures to be covered in more depth.

Inclusion in the early years

Government initiatives such as the *Special Educational Needs Code of Practice* (DfES, 2001d) and the Special Educational Needs and Disability Discrimination Act 2001 (DfES, 2001c) were intended to lead to a more inclusive educational system. The Code of Practice (DfES, 2001d) gives specific guidance on the procedures practitioners need to follow when special needs are suspected or identified. Children with special needs are not necessarily children with learning difficulties. Having special needs means that there might be factors which prevent children from achieving their full potential. These impediments need to be removed or the child may need to be given support in overcoming such barriers to learning. Meeting the diverse needs of children is one of the principles for early years education expressed in the *Curriculum Guidance for the Foundation Stage* (QCA, 2000b). Practitioners are expected to be aware of the legislation related to planning and teaching for:

- boys and girls;
- children with special educational needs;
- children who are more able;
- children with disabilities;
- children from all social, cultural and religious backgrounds;
- children of different ethnic groups including travellers, refugees and asylum seekers; and
- children from diverse linguistic backgrounds.

Not all children from these groups will have special needs related to language and literacy learning. However, they might. The research has consistently shown that boys underachieve in reading and writing when compared with girls and that this may start to become evident in the early years. Boys may be less interested in activities associated with reading and writing and tend to choose activities which are physical rather than contemplative. Special educational needs come in many forms including behavioural, emotional and social needs. However, children who are withdrawn, disruptive, hyperactive or who are unable to concentrate are likely to find it difficult to learn to read and write, and their behaviour may mean that they get less practice at developing their use of language for social purposes or to think and learn. More able children often demonstrate their ability through oral language. They are often articulate and can use oral language to reason, explain and question. They will need to be challenged and stretched so that their ability continues to grow. Children with disabilities such as hearing and visual impairments could be disadvantaged in learning oral and written language unless special account is taken of their physical needs. Being aware of the values, expectations and traditions of different social, cultural, religious and ethnic groups will influence the topics that are planned and the resources, including books, that are used. If we want to make learning relevant to all children and capitalize on their home and community learning, we need to be aware of what this might include. Thought needs to be given to the needs of children who are acquiring English as an additional language in order for them to learn both the oral and written versions of English. Being aware that many children may have special needs, if they are to realize their potential as learners, can help practitioners to anticipate their needs and plan carefully in order to accommo-date them.

Inclusive teaching

Inclusive teaching has three elements each of which can be adjusted to take account of children's needs (DfES, 2002):

- overcoming potential barriers to learning;
- setting suitable learning challenges; and
- responding to pupils' diverse needs.

When all three have been adapted it is likely that practice will be inclusive. This is illustrated in Figure 5.1 where inclusion is represented as the overlap at the tip of the arrow.

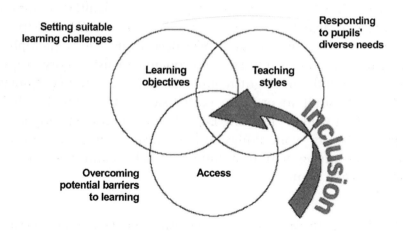

Figure 5.1 *The circles of inclusion (DfES, 2002)*

Overcoming potential barriers to learning

The starting point for removing barriers to learning is to respect and value all children. Staff in an inclusive setting provide an environment where children of different races, gender, social class and learning need are recognized and regarded positively. The language that practitioners use will reflect their focus on the child first and their special need second. They will talk about a child who is from a traveller background rather than a traveller child. They will undertake regular training and professional development to ensure that they learn about different types of special need and keep up to date with ways of enabling all children to learn to make progress.

Difficulties in learning can arise from an unsuitable environment, such as unsuitable teaching methods, or inaccessible curriculum materials as well as from individual children's needs. It is possible to make the classroom environment more conducive to supporting children with special needs. Soft surfaces, cushions and carpets help to absorb noise and make it easier for everyone to hear clearly. Pictures as well as words can be used to label storage areas to help children who cannot read. Pictures and books which portray positive images of people with disabilities and positive representations of girls and boys engaged in a range of non-stereotypical behaviours, and story tapes in the languages that are spoken by the children, should form some of the resources that are used for communication, language and literacy. Multisensory and interactive books are helpful for children with visual impairments or those who lack concentration.

Staff may need to plan specific access strategies that will help all children to learn. They will need to anticipate the potential difficulties children may have and make arrangements to overcome them. For children with communication or visual problems, staff may need to use radio microphones, use large-print texts and keep story times concrete by using story props and visual aids. Some children might require specialist aids and equipment or support from an adult in order to participate in the activities that are planned. Children who are learning English as an additional language will need opportunities to work alongside English-speaking peers and adults. They might also receive help from bilingual teachers and this will need to be considered when planning.

Activity

Would you like to be known as 'someone with glasses' or 'the one with brown hair' or would you prefer to be identified as 'someone who loves to dance' or ' a person who knows about science'? Think about how you refer to children. Would you like to be referred to in this way? Do shorthand descriptions narrow the picture we have of children or are they positive and empowering?

Setting suitable learning challenges

Learning objectives can be taken from the stepping stones or Early Learning Goals that are easier or harder than those set for the majority of children. They should be at an appropriate level for the child to succeed. Sometimes learning objectives and tasks are not adapted. Instead, a teaching or learning assistant might help the child to complete the work. While this is sometimes helpful it is not always the best solution, as the activity may be inappropriate and in order to complete it the adult may do most of the work.

Responding to pupils' diverse needs

Teaching styles are selected because they are motivating and appropriate to the needs of the children. Teachers may use a range of methods suited to visual, auditory and kinaesthetic learners. They may design shorter tasks for children who find it difficult to concentrate or more open-ended tasks or complex tasks for more able children.

Play, which is central to teaching and learning in early years, offers an ideal vehicle for responding to children's individual needs and can make a significant contribution to their learning. The following example shows how staff in a nursery responded to the complex needs of one child by allowing her to play.

Umay was a 4-year-old child. She entered the nursery class part way through the spring term. Her parents were Turkish. They were applying for refugee status and had left Turkey in difficult circumstances. Initially when they left Turkey they had left Umay behind to be looked after by her grandmother. Umay had only just rejoined her parents when she began at the nursery. Umay spoke only Turkish. Her parents had a limited knowledge and understanding of English.

When she started in the nursery Umay manifested some difficult anti-social behaviours. She was aggressive and destructive. Without provocation she pinched and hit other children and often destroyed their work. She also damaged classroom resources. Her lack of English meant that it was difficult to discover what was troubling her or to reason with her. Any classroom activities such as story times or discussions were difficult for her, both because of her behaviour and because of her lack of understanding of what was said. Umay was a frustrated child who was manifesting a range of needs. She was behaviourally difficult, emotionally needy and was unable to interact socially with others. One of the contributing factors to this list of difficulties was Umay's lack of English but her difficulties went beyond this. They also interfered with some of the normal strategies for helping Umay's second language to develop. She was not listening to others talking or listening to stories and she often ripped up reading books and paper when adults tried to read or write with her.

The staff of the nursery made an application to the local education authority to have Umay's needs assessed but there was a delay before the appropriate staff could see her. The school had the services of a visiting Turkish teacher once a week but Umay's behaviour made it hard for her to take advantage of his sessions. In the meantime, staff had to try and cater for Umay's needs and help her to integrate into the class.

The only thing that Umay wanted to do when she came into class was to play in the role-play area. Here she would become engrossed in tidying, sorting and cleaning, and would tenderly care for the dolls and soft toys. For a week or so Umay was allowed to play alone in the role-play area for long periods. During this time she was calm and caring. She was also willing to allow an adult to play alongside her for some of the time. This was a good opportunity to talk to Umay and in so doing model English and begin to establish a relationship with her.

The nursery staff capitalized on Umay's interest in domestic play by creating a separate role-play area for her use. They made a small home corner as Umay transformed any role play into a home. The other children had their usual and varied role-play provision. After about a week in this new play area Umay was invited to create some materials for the house such as making wallpaper and pictures in the art area and making food and sweets for the dolls out of play dough. To do this Umay had to be near to other children as she worked and she was exposed to their language use. She was also gaining skills and confidence in using a more varied set of resources and tools. All these activities were not problem-free. Umay occasionally made sorties into the main role-play area to kidnap dolls and appropriate other resources, and she could also be destructive of other children's art work.

By the end of the summer term Umay had calmed down a great deal. She was willing to undertake a variety of activities in the classroom. She could, for short periods, work and play with other children. Sometimes she invited other children to play with her in her house. She listened to stories and even read books to the dolls. She began to explore mark-making by making greeting cards and postcards for the dolls. Her use of English was beginning to develop, she could identify objects and communicate generally through the use of single words or phrases. She also seemed to be much happier and more settled.

Play had helped Umay socially, behaviourally and cognitively. Although by the end of the year Umay continued to have special educational needs, she had made significant progress. The staff had provided resources that were appropriate to Umay's interests and through careful planning and sensitive interaction they were able to cater for her needs and develop her abilities. Most importantly, Umay was now much more willing and motivated to learn.

In order to cater for Umay's special educational needs staff drew upon all three aspects of inclusive practice. They responded to her needs by initially drawing back from any direct teaching. By allowing her to play, Umay was able to develop the skills that she found difficult when she was with other people. In her home corner she was calm, was able to demonstrate awareness of the feelings she attributed to the dolls, such as unhappiness and hunger, and she interacted with the toys by talking and singing to them. Many of the barriers to learning were Umay's own emotional and social difficulties, and to remove these she needed a safe place and unthreatening activities. To give her access to learning she was given her own special resources. The staff were concerned that Umay did learn during her time in the nursery. They were aware that Umay's learning involved social development as well as academic learning. Through observations and team discussions they planned opportunities to extend Umay's interaction with others and to engage in language and literacy activities.

Effective teaching is teaching that it responsive to children's needs and so, 'Effective education for children with SEN shares most of the characteristics of effective teaching for all children' (DfES, 2004c: para 3.2). It involves:

- having high expectations of all children;
- building on the knowledge, interests and aptitudes of every child;
- involving children in their own learning;
- helping children to become confident learners; and
- enabling children to develop the skills they will need beyond the immediate context.

Identification of special educational needs

Before entry to nursery or reception

Some young children who have significant and long-term needs or disabilities will already have had these identified before they start in nursery or reception classes. In this case, practitioners will want to use the existing information to make the child's entry as smooth as possible. A joint planning meeting involving parents, any professionals who have been involved with the child and the family, the teacher and the special educational needs coordinator can be a good start. Parents and other professionals might be able to provide teachers with contact details for national organizations or other sources of information. This is particularly helpful if the special need is unfamiliar to the school. This will help practitioners understand the practical implications of the special need and help them to prepare. Depending on the nature of the special need, the child might be invited to visit the class after the children have left. This is an opportunity for the child to meet the adults who work there and it also gives staff the chance to learn about any special equipment the child may use.

Findings from the Effective Provision of Pre-school Education (EPPE) project (www.ioe.ac.uk/projects/eppe) and the associated Early Years Transitions and SEN (EYTSEN) (Sammons et al., 2003) project suggest that early years education has a positive effect on young children's cognitive development. When they started pre-school, one-third of the sample of children tracked were identified as being at risk in terms of their cognitive development, but by the time they started primary school, only one-fifth were. The researchers concluded that pre-school can be an effective intervention for reducing SEN, especially for the most disadvantaged and vulnerable children. This is very encouraging news for Foundation Stage practitioners.

In nursery and reception

Some children's special educational needs only become apparent once the child has started in nursery or reception. The staff's observations and assessments of pupils' progress might alert them to potential difficulties.

During the Foundation Stage children will progress at different rates. By the end of the stage, some will have achieved beyond the expectations set out in the *Curriculum Guidance for the Foundation Stage* (QCA, 2000b) and others may still be working towards the Early Learning Goals. Not all children who are making slower progress will have special educational needs, although they may need to have carefully differentiated learning opportunities to help them progress and practitioners will monitor their progress carefully. A child who has special educational needs has difficulties that are significant, and is defined as a child who, despite receiving appropriate early educational experiences:

- makes little or no progress even when teaching approaches are particularly targeted to improve the child's identified areas of weakness;
- continues working at levels significantly below those expected for children of a similar age in certain areas;
- presents persistent emotional and/or behavioural difficulties, which are not ameliorated by the behaviour management techniques usually employed in the setting;
- has sensory or physical problems, and continues to make little or no progress despite the provision of personal aids and equipment; and
- has communication and/or interaction difficulties, and requires specific individual interventions in order to access learning (DfES, 2001d: para. 4.21).

This may mean that the child remains at the level of the first stepping stone of learning while other children have developed further. This lack of progress continues despite a differentiated curriculum and support being given to the child. Although practitioners may have concerns about a child during the first term in the nursery or reception class, it is unlikely that they would definitely consider the child as having special needs at this time. It is sensible to allow the child to settle into the new setting and benefit from the activities and experiences before making a judgement. During their observations of such children, practitioners will be looking for signs of progress as well as noting things which suggest that the child may have problems.

Managing special educational needs

When, despite quality teaching and a suitably differentiated curriculum, children do not appear to be making progress in their learning, it is necessary to move on to the next stage of meeting their needs through special educational provision 'which is additional to, or otherwise different from, the educational provision made generally for children of their age in schools' (DfES, 2001d: para. 1.3). This will in the first instance be planned for through Early Years Action and, if that does not result in progress, Early Years Action Plus.

Early Years Action

The triggers for Early Years Action are the practitioners' concerns or the concerns of parents. They may have evidence that, despite the child receiving differentiated learning opportunities, progress is still not satisfactory. Early Years Action means that interventions that are additional or different to those provided for other children are necessary. These are over and above the normal differentiated curriculum. At this stage an Individual Education Plan will be drawn up. This states the action that will be taken to help the child progress. It will contain information about the nature of the child's learning difficulties, short-term targets set for the child, the teaching strategies and the provision to be put in place, when the plan is to be reviewed, and the outcome of the action taken. The Individual Education Plan should only record that which is additional to or different from the normal differentiated curriculum and provision that are in place. It is crisply written and focuses on three or four key targets. The plan is drawn up after consultation between the special educational needs coordinator, teachers, the pupil and parents. Individual Education Plans are monitored regularly and frequently, and are reviewed three times a year. Parents are consulted as part of the review. An example of an Individual Educational plan is given in Figure 5.2.

Early Years Action Plus

In cases where Early Years Action does not result in the child making sufficient progress, Early Years Action Plus may be necessary. The trigger for Early Years Action Plus is a continued lack of progress in spite of Early Years Action. Decisions about future action are then made by the special educational needs coordinator and practitioners. Parents are consulted and involved in decisions about what should happen next. External support

Individual Education Plan

Early Years Action

Name: Amy
Date of Birth: 26.05.01
Areas of concern: Verbal comprehension and expressive language

Start date: January 2006
Review date: 10.03.06

Targets	Resources	Activities	Outcome
1 Develop understanding of opposites	Sorting materials Caption and picture books	Play games involving sorting and matching using vocabulary related to opposites such as big, small, up, down, fast, slow, etc. Share books with Amy. Some of these could be caption books containing concepts related to opposites.	
2 Develop confidence in using language	Learning support assistant	Work with LSA as a talking partner. Encourage her to make contributions in groups after she has had time to rehearse or think about what she wants to say.	
3 Use expressive language with understanding in particular, vocabulary related to opposites, adjectives and the correct use of the past tense	Role-play areas Craft activities Matching and sorting games	Include Amy in role play as much as possible. Make sure she plays with supportive friends. Model language use while playing and working alongside Amy In painting and collage and other creative activities encourage Amy's use of language with particular attention to opposites, adjectives and past tense.	

Figure 5.2 *An Individual Educational Plan*

services are usually involved at this stage as they can help with advice on designing new Individual Education Plans and targets, provide more specialist assessments, give advice on the use of new or specialist strategies or materials, and in some cases provide support for particular activities.

Where an early education setting seeks the help of external support services, those services will need to see the records that have been made in order to establish which strategies have already been employed and which targets have been set and achieved. They will usually then observe the child, in their educational setting if that is appropriate and practicable, as this helps them to tailor their advice to the child's needs.

Statutory assessment

A very small proportion of children have long-term difficulties. In these cases, where the help given through Early Years Action and Early Years Action Plus has not enabled the child to make adequate progress, practitioners can request a statutory assessment for a Statement of Special Educational Need. Where a request for statutory assessment is made to a local education authority, the child will have demonstrated significant cause for concern. Practitioners will need to provide evidence that the strategies or programme implemented for the child have been continued for a reasonable period of time without success.

Special educational needs in communication, language and literacy

Special educational needs are usually defined as falling into one or more of the following areas:

- communication and interaction;
- cognition and learning;
- behaviour, emotional and social development; and
- sensory and/or physical.

Communication and interaction needs include speech and language delay, impairments and disorders, dyslexia and hearing impairment. It is usually too early to identify dyslexia in children during the Foundation Stage as many of its characteristics are typical of children's early reading and writing behaviour (Tassoni, 2003). Examples of sensory and physical needs include hearing impairment and visual impairment. Ways of working with children who have difficulties with oral language or who have a hearing or visual impairment are discussed in Chapter 2.

Conditions within all four types of special educational need are likely to interfere with a child's ability to make progress in communication, language and literacy. Behaviour, emotional and social problems may arise as secondary conditions when children have other learning difficulties, particularly those relating to communication, language and literacy. They can become 'frustrated at not being understood and develop behaviour difficulties ... Unfortunately, the aggressive behaviour may gain adult attention and subsequent referral for support, leaving the primary underlying language difficulty unnoticed' (Martin, 2000: 10).

Boys and girls

The gender gap in literacy

Each year, when the results of the national tests for English at Key Stages 1 and 2 are published, concern is expressed about the lower level of achievement of boys when compared to girls. We also know that boys, as a group, tend to have less favourable attitudes to literacy than girls (HMI, 2004). Underachievement and less favourable attitudes begin early and, although there is less evidence in the Foundation Stage, they need to be addressed at the start of children's education.

Causes of boys' underachievement

A survey of the literature related to boys and underachievement (Younger et al., 2005) found that a number of explanations had been proposed. These were:

- the biological construction of masculinity and brain differences between girls and boys;
- boys' disregard for authority, academic work and formal achievement, and attitudes that are in conflict with the ethos of school;
- gender differences in attitudes to work, and their goals and aspirations linked to the wider social context of changing labour markets, de-industrialization and male unemployment;
- girls' increased maturity and more effective learning strategies including collaboration, talk and sharing, whilst boys were seen as less willing to collaborate to learn and use cooperative talk and discussion to support their own learning;

- differential gender interactions between pupils and teachers in the classroom; and
- the importance for boys of being accepted by their male peers, which might involve adopting laddish behaviour and rejecting school norms and learning.

Some of these factors might have a direct application to children in the Foundation Stage, for example, teachers having different expectations of boys and girls as learners. However, all will have an impact on the models of attitudes to and use of language and literacy that young boys see in their families and communities. Millard (2003) suggests that because it is mothers and older sisters who share books with children and who involve children in writing, literacy becomes feminized in the eyes of young learners. She suggests that because boys in Western cultures tend to reject activities that are seen as girl appropriate, they are less likely to be interested in literacy than girls.

Thinking about girls

Whilst, currently, it is the underachievement of boys that is receiving attention, it is important not to forget about girls and their needs. Although girls might perceive reading and writing as activities that are appropriate to them, not all girls succeed easily and not all of them do as well as they could. In comparison with boys, girls tend to be more passive and take fewer risks in their learning than boys. They are more accepting of the tasks that they are given in school. As a result they might spend a great deal of time on writing in order to get it right. This can mean that they become preoccupied with how their writing looks rather than what it says. They can become anxious about correct spelling and handwriting, rather than experimenting with content and style and finding out about what writing can do. Girls may need to be challenged to do better at literacy in case they too underachieve.

Ways of improving boys' attitudes and success

Although many of the factors which contribute to boys' underachievement exist outside the classroom, there are a number of things that practitioners can do to help boys become more interested in language and literacy and to become more successful. These activities are also appropriate and beneficial for girls. These include:

- using a variety of interactive and well-paced teaching methods which capture the children's interest;
- planning literacy sessions which are imaginative and varied;
- using talk, role play and small-world play to prepare for and support writing;
- making use of response partners to give children a chance to gather and try out ideas before writing and to get feedback on written work;
- making use of ICT for writing so that the presentation of writing is good and changes to writing can be made easily;
- making use of tape recorders for children to record final versions of their writing;
- giving children the opportunity to write using a range of writing types such as speech bubbles, captions and labels;
- making sure that all the writing that children are asked to do is necessary, purposeful and relevant to them, if evidence of curriculum coverage is needed making sure that this is gained through photographs, diagrams or pictures rather than through writing;
- making the purpose of pieces of writing and the outcome of any writing that is produced clear;
- linking reading and writing to role play, games and construction activities;
- knowing what reading material children like to read for example, comics or books on particular topics and providing this for them; and
- providing peer support for reading by pairing boys and girls from Key Stage 1 with boys and girls in the Foundation Stage.

The keys to success in communication, language and literacy are motivation, interest and satisfaction. If boys and girls experience a curriculum that is imaginative, varied and relevant to their interests and needs, they are more likely to achieve well.

Activity

Audit the activities boys choose in the nursery and reception class and observe their involvement with self-selected or adult-led literacy activities. Talk to any children who seem disengaged about why this might be. Use the information to inform future planning for communication, language and literacy.

More able children

Children who are developing significantly ahead of their age demonstrate advanced cognitive behaviours and sophisticated ways of learning. They have more knowledge and acquire it in a qualitatively different way compared with average learners. Where the giftedness is in the area of communication, language and literacy they may show many of the following characteristics:

- comprehend language early;
- use advanced speech in terms of vocabulary, grammar and clear articulation;
- use metaphors and analogies;
- make up songs or stories spontaneously;
- modify their language to suit less mature children;
- use language for a real exchange of ideas and information at an early age; and
- carry out instructions to do several things in succession (Porter, 2002: 261–2).

Children who are gifted and talented need the opportunity to develop their thinking, understanding and learning. This can be done by giving them open-ended tasks and activities which involve analysis, reasoning or problem-solving. For example, they might be able to sequence a set of pictures to retell a story without help from an adult. They could then extend the sequence by making pictures which depict a prequel as well as a sequel and be asked to talk about their decisions. While gifted children often enjoy working independently, they benefit from conversations with adults. It is important that these are conversations, not question and answer sessions where the child's ability is being assessed. This dialogue between children and adults is important for all children, and examples of productive adult and child talk are given in Chapter 2. Gifted children might be reading in advance of the expectations for their age. It is not necessary to give them harder books to read or introduce them to a formal phonic programme. It is the quality of their understanding of books, characters, events and language that are important. Again discussion will support the expression of their understanding and help to develop their knowledge.

Children acquiring English as an additional language

Children who are learning English as an additional language (EAL) are not a homogeneous group. They have a variety of linguistic, cultural and ethnic backgrounds. Some children will have been born in this country, and although they may have been exposed to some English in their homes and the wider community, it is not their first and most fluent language. Some children may have recently arrived in this country either because their parents are working or studying here or have left their country of origin as refugees.

Gathering information

When children first enter the setting, practitioners need to know which language or languages the child understands and speaks and what experience the child has had with the written form of the language. This can help practitioners provide appropriate resources such as dual-language books. It will also help them to become familiar with the conventions and scripts that are used, and they will be able to see if this is reflected in the child's early writing. Edwards (2004) has written a useful book which lists the characteristics of many languages spoken or encountered by bilingual learners.

Teaching approaches

The Foundation Stage provides children with an ideal environment in which to learn English. The practical and play-based curriculum provides children with the visible prompts which makes what is being said understandable. Bilingual children benefit from seeing practical demonstrations of what they are expected to do and from visual support such as that provided by real objects and pictures. The emphasis on oral language also provides children with lots of opportunities to hear and try out English. When talking to bilingual learners, keeping eye contact and using gesture can help practitioners to establish what the child understands and clarify what is being said.

Most schools will have the services of a visiting teacher who can work with EAL learners for some time each week. Specialist teachers generally work with the children in the classroom helping them to access the activities and learning that has been planned. This involves careful planning and liaison between the class teacher and the EAL teacher. Seeing and discussing the strategies that specialists use can be helpful as these methods can be incorporated into the teacher's practice when specialist support is not available. Because EAL teachers only spend a limited amount of time in each school, it is the class teacher who has the main responsibility for helping the children learn English.

Oral language

When learning a new language, learners go through a number of stages which are similar to those observed in first language learning which was described in Chapter 2. The first stage is a silent period. During this stage the learner is listening intently to the unfamiliar language, identifying particular sounds and words and trying to link these to situations and objects. At this stage the child will be learning a great deal but will lack the confidence and the experience to say anything. During the silent period children need to hear as much language as possible. In order to give children at this stage the opportunity to join in with activities and demonstrate their understanding, practitioners can ask questions that can be answered with non-verbal responses. Children will make use of non-verbal forms of communication to make their needs known and to join in with others. As children become more confident with the new language they will begin to talk. At first they will use single words such as, *OK, me, paint.* Gradually they begin to produce two- and three-word utterances such as *where you go?*, which follow the word order and structure of English. This is followed by complete sentences and more complex sentences. Conversational fluency, meaning the ability to use high-frequency words and simple grammatical constructions, takes about two years to develop in a second language (Cummins, 2000). Native speakers of English generally develop conversational fluency by the age of 5. Cognitive and academic language proficiency, the sort of language needed to understand and discuss complex ideas, takes much longer to develop, so even if a child seems to be fluent in English they may still need support in developing their second language further.

Reading and writing

Young bilingual learners need the same opportunities as monolingual children to hear stories and share books with adults. The illustrations in books provide children with an excellent visual support for the words they are hearing and listening to, and the same language of the book repeated a number of times helps them to acquire vocabulary in context. They also need the same opportunities to experiment with writing as all other children. Children who have had experience of seeing writing in their home language may incorporate into their early writing the forms they have seen or used. Demonstrations of writing, and discussions about it, will help children as they learn about the English writing system. Shared reading and shared writing are particularly helpful to children learning to read and write in English.

An inclusive environment

Helping children to recognize that there are many different ways of seeing and understanding the world is an important dimension of learning. These different ways depend on a range of social, cultural and religious and ethnic viewpoints. Children's self-image is enhanced when their cultural heritage, gender, beliefs and the lifestyles of their families are respected, acknowledged and used in the planning of educational experiences and activities. Taking account of the interests and skills emerging from the diversity that children and their families bring to the early years setting enriches and extends learning.

Activities and the use of resources that encourage cultural awareness can be integrated into various types of play including role play, in activities associated with music and books, in preparing foods from different cultures and in celebrating religious and cultural festivals. Books, pictures, jigsaws, stories, rhymes and puzzles should be selected to show positive images of people of different races and cultures, and show girls, boys, men and women in a range of roles. The creation of a stimulating visual environment in which there are photographs, paintings, prints and textiles reflecting different cultural traditions can also reflect the diversity of Britain.

Activity

Make a collection of stories and rhymes from each of the five continents of the world, Africa, America (North and South), Asia, Australasia and Europe. How could you use this collection with children aged between 3 and 5 years?

Conclusion

Catering for the individual needs of children is demanding and exacting. However, it is the basis of good teaching and is essential if all children are to get the education that they require and deserve. In this chapter I have outlined a range of inclusive practices, procedures and activities which practitioners adopt in order to meet the diverse needs of children who attend early years settings.

 Further reading

Mortimer, H. (2001) *Special Needs and Early Years Provision*. London: Continuum.
A detailed and practical overview of how to identify and cater for special educational needs in the Foundation Stage.

Porter, L. (2002) *Educating Young Children with Special Educational Needs*. London: Paul Chapman Publishing.

A very thorough examination of a the special educational needs that practitioners may encounter. It contains lots of practical suggestions about provision and teaching.

Primary National Strategy (PNS) (2005) *Boys' Writing Flyers*. London: DfES.
These contain some useful ideas about activities which will interest boys in reading and writing in the Foundation Stage.

Sutherland, M. (2005) *Gifted and Talented in the Early Years*. London: Paul Chapman Publishing.
This contains suggestions about age-appropriate activities which can be offered to young gifted and talented children.

Tassoni, P. (2003) *Supporting Special Needs: Understanding Inclusion in the Early Years*. Oxford: Heinemann Educational Publishers.
This is a detailed and practical book covering all aspects of identifying and providing for children with special educational needs in the Foundation Stage.

Websites

Many organizations concerned with special needs have informative websites:

www.rnib.org.uk, Royal National Institute for the Blind.
www.look-uk.org, National Federation of Families with Visually Impaired Children.
www.rnid.org.uk, Royal National Institute for the Deaf.
www.ndcs.org.uk, The National Deaf Children's Society.
www.nasen.org.uk, National Association for Special Educational Needs.

There are also some useful websites to consult if you are working with EAL pupils:

www.becta.org.uk/teachers/display.cfm?section=1-3-2, the British Educational Communications and Technology Agency has information about translation engines as well as information from community language teachers, advice sheets and software sites.
www.naldic.org.uk/ITTSEAL, the National Association for Language Development in the Curriculum is the professional association of EAL teachers. It contains information about EAL pedagogy, practice, policies, research and resources. The ITTSEAL section is specifically aimed at Initial Teacher Education (ITE).
www.multiverse.ac.uk, the Multiverse website contains a wide range of recommended online material on issues of diversity: race and ethnicity, social class, religion, bilingual learners, travellers and refugees, specifically for ITE.

Chapter 6

Working with parents and other adults

Introduction

Practitioners in the Foundation Stage are members of a team which consists of professionals and non-professionals. In order to work well with others they need to have good interpersonal skills. They also need to understand and value the skills that their co-workers have. Parents play a significant part in the education and care of their children. They too are part of the Foundation Stage team. This chapter explores the roles of all concerned with children in the Foundation Stage and makes some suggestions about how practitioners can work effectively with them.

Definitions of parental involvement

There is a well-established tradition of practitioners working with parents and carers in the Foundation Stage but the ways in which professionals and parents work together are diverse. Parents have been variously termed 'clients', 'resources', 'participants' or 'partners' by educationalists. The notion of the parent as client is now rather outdated. As clients, parents are characterized as being dependent upon the opinions of experts, passive in their receipt of services, in need of redirection, peripheral to decision-making and inadequate or deficient. The term 'resource' implies that parents can be useful. They may have a skill that can benefit the school or the children. As participants, parents may be regarded as potential participants in school-designed programmes or activities such as reading with children at home or in school. Partnership means that professionals respect and act on the knowledge and understanding that parents have of their individual children as well as acknowledging their interest in their child's education and involvement in it at home. It means that parents recognize that staff know about children, their development and their learning. They respect the expertise of professionals and know that this will be used to benefit all children. Parents and teachers have complementary but different roles as educators. While some parents may act as resources and participants at times, partnership is what schools are aiming for. In partnership, mutual respect and the sharing of information are key. The discussions that professionals and parents have may lead to action. For example, teachers might plan work that they know will appeal to children, or parents might extend some of the work children have engaged in at school. They might talk about and look more intently at buildings in the locality if children have been learning about their environment. However, such actions grow from a shared understanding of children's learning needs and what counts as education.

Learning at home

Parents contribute to children's learning in many ways. We know from a number of research studies that many parents contribute in direct and visible ways to their children's literacy learning through providing children with resources for reading and writing, models of literacy in use and opportunities to engage in language and literacy practices (Tizard and Hughes, 2002; Weinberger, 1996). However, homes can provide children with more than the opportunity to practise literacy in conventional ways (Wolfendale, 2000). Children's values and attitudes are learned at home. These include valuing learning and developing attitudes to education and schooling. Positive attitudes to school and belief in oneself as a learner can make a significant contribution to educational success. Homes also provide children with a curriculum which consists of conversations, activities, outings and hobbies, and where learning and teaching can be spontaneous, flexible and prolonged.

The nature of literacy has changed rapidly in recent years. Word processing, e-mail, text messaging, the Internet, television and video have expanded our understanding of what it means to be literate. Homes provide children with their induction into these experiences of literacy. In her research into young children's home-based literacy practices, Marsh (2004: 53) found that, 'a range of popular cultural texts such as computers (mainly console) games, comics, books based on television characters and environmental print linked to media texts (stickers, video labels, computer game boxes and so on)' were part of most children's out of school literacy experiences. Such knowledge of children's literacy learning at home can be beneficial to teachers, as it provides us with information about what interests children. It can help practitioners to think of ways to build on existing knowledge and provide motivating ways of extending learning. Using children's interests and resources with which they are familiar, such as comics or videos, helps children to feel confident and embeds learning in contexts which make sense to them. It is also helpful as children are likely to enter the Foundation Stage with an understanding of some of the real-life uses of reading and writing, and an awareness of the relevance and place of literacy in their lives. Both of which are key parts of the language and literacy curriculum in the Foundation Stage.

Finding out about children's experiences at home before and outside school is an important aspect of planning and teaching. We know that children make most progress when there is some congruency between their experiences at home and in school. Consequently, practitioners need to know as much as possible about what and how children have learned. This is the first step in establishing a partnership with parents. Staff need to get and act on information from parents about their children as well as provide parents with information about school, the curriculum and their child's progress. Children benefit when both parties receive and give information.

Partnership and disadvantage

Now may be the time to rethink why we want to involve parents in schools and learning, and to consider our approach. In terms of offering equal opportunities to all children, it might be particularly important to think about the form of parental involvement that is most beneficial. Most partnership programmes are mainly concerned with encouraging parents to participate in school-initiated learning such as reading with children at home. While this can be an enjoyable activity for parents and children, and has benefits for children's reading development, as the main form of parental involvement it is may be outdated. Many parents regularly share books with their children at home (Tizard and Hughes, 2002; Weinberger, 1996) and so this does not extend parents' involvement in education. Such programmes serve to prioritize conventional forms of literacy such as book-based reading and pencil-and-paper representation, and it is now recognized that there are many other forms of literacy. Finally, asking parents to act as agents of the school by participating in school-initiated parental involvement programmes is less likely to benefit children from disadvantaged homes and, indeed, could doubly disadvantage them. Research studies suggest that children who achieve well and those whose parents have a high level of understanding of literacy and schooling are probably least in need of additional help at home but their parents are most likely to become involved in home school programmes (Desforges and Abouchaar, 2003; Edwards and Warin, 1999). This is not an argument against school-initiated parental involvement but a question about how best partnership with parents can be used to the advantage of children who might benefit most from it.

Activity

Imagine a school where parents are visible. They might be helping in classrooms or involved in fund-raising. There may be an assumption that the school has a good relationship with parents. Is this really the case? Ask yourself, which parents come into the school? Is it always the same ones? If it is, why is this? Is it because, either overtly or covertly, some parents are deemed more acceptable or suitable?

Ways of working with parents

Effective working relationships are built on respect and understanding. Parents need to feel welcomed and valued by staff. The role that they have played and continue to play in their child's education needs to be acknowledged. Schools need to have procedures which facilitate a two-way flow of information between home and school in order for schools to build on the learning that takes place at home and for parents to extend school learning in ways that are appropriate to their own child and their own circumstances. Some suggestions about how to establish effective relationships with parents and focus the exchange of information on learning are given below.

Respecting parents

- Ask parents, perhaps through a questionnaire, what they would like to know about how to help their children with communication, language and literacy at home.
- Partnership can also be strengthened by encouraging parents to see themselves as active and valued members of the early years community, involved in day-to-day learning experiences, planning and participating in events and visits, organizing social events and helping to raise funds for specific projects.
- From the time parents register their child with the school or nursery, include them in invitations to use the toy and book library, attend special school events and use the parents' room.

- Make sure you know about each family's cultural, language and religious background.

Receiving information

- The starting point for this is the pre-entry visit to the early years setting. As well as welcoming and familiarizing children and parents with the setting, this provides an opportunity to involve parents and children in discussion about the child's achievements to date.
- If possible parents should be involved in settling children into the early years setting. The process is eased where parents are welcome to stay and play with the children until their child is confident with staff and other children. This also assists staff discussion with parents of how their child is settling into their new setting.
- Particularly in reception classes, parents can become involved in the first activity of the day. This gives them the opportunity to see and understand what children do when they are away from home.
- Organize a regular slot when teachers are available to meet with parents to discuss their children's progress and needs.
- Parents are encouraged to contribute to their child's Foundation Stage Profile. Meeting to discuss this and other termly meetings to discuss and record children's progress provide opportunities for parents to share information.

Giving general information about school and learning

- Displays of children's work and photographs with captions explaining the learning gained from activities and experiences will help to share the aims of education with parents.
- Clear and well-presented written communication in a prospectus or handbook and newsletters can keep parents up to date. Where possible these should be provided in the different languages used by parents.
- Video some sessions and activities for parents so that they can see what goes on in nursery and reception. The video could include adults sharing and talking about books with children. These can be copied onto a DVD and given to each child to take home.
- Develop a school website for parents.
- Set up a parents' room with a library of books, toys and games that parents can borrow.
- Organize curriculum fairs and workshops where parents gain genuine

insight into how things are being taught. For example, children's work can be displayed and the children can explain what they have been doing.

- Send newsletters home both hard copies and by e-mail.

Giving information about individual children

- Regular informal contacts as children are brought to the early years setting and collected are useful for exchanging information about children.
- Open days and meetings can provide a useful opportunity to discuss the curriculum with parents. An important focus of such meetings should be to reaffirm the contribution of parents to their children's learning and to suggest ways of supporting learning at home.
- It is good practice to provide oral reports to parents (for example, after children have settled in and again towards the end of a year) and a written report on their progress and achievement.
- Save pieces of work, photographs of models and the child at work on a CD-ROM to send home at the end of the year.

> ### Activity
> Do you find it easier to work with some parents rather than others? Why is this? Which kind of parents are these? Are they more like you in terms of their values and ways of thinking? What are the implications?

Involving parents in communication, language and literacy at home

Some parents are eager to help their children at home and ask staff how best to do this. Before offering suggestions it is wise to find out what parents already do so that we can make suggestions that are new rather than repeating what they already know. As Weinberger's (1996) research showed, many parents will already be reading and sharing books and involving children in literacy events in the home and the community. What follows is a list of ideas which are not expensive and require no special knowledge. If there are things on this list that parents are not doing and would like to do these can be offered as suggestions.

What all parents can do

- Watch videos of children's stories together.
- Encourage children's attempts to read and write.

- Help children with simple word puzzles in activity books.
- Share bedtime stories with children.
- Join in with children's imaginative play by writing lists and signs.
- Enter into word play by making up rhyming words with children.
- Help children to make up their own illustrated books.
- Share books with children.
- Tell improvised stories during car or bus journeys.
- Listen to children read aloud from a book they have brought from school.
- Read letters and greetings cards to children.
- Read aloud from the television listings or teletext.
- Refer to a recipe when children are helping with cooking.
- Write letters and names in sand, on misty window panes and other surfaces.
- Provide children with pencils, mugs and other items which bear their name.
- Ask children to help during shopping trips by finding items on the shelves.
- Sing nursery rhymes together.
- Take children to the library.
- Take children to book shops.
- Provide children with pencils, crayons and paper.
- Provide children with playthings such as magnetic and plastic letters.
- Let children watch adults write.
- Look at websites and computer programs together.
- Borrow books, story tapes and story sacks.
- Read books, comics, magazines and catalogues with children.
- Watch and talk about television programmes such as *Words and Pictures* and *The Tweenies*.

Involving the parents of pupils learning English as an additional language

Bilingual parents can become involved in their children's learning in the same ways as parents of solely English-speaking children. In addition, they may be able to make a particular contribution to the school or setting and, if they are willing, they can be asked to contribute towards the resources of the class by:

- recording stories onto audio and video tape;
- recording rhymes and songs on tape;

- contributing to dual language story sacks
- translating labels, signs, notices, letters and class books;
- writing first language versions of popular books, stories and poems; and
- bringing written material from home into the setting.

We need to take care not just to see bilingual parents as a resource for school-based literacy. Translation services and language support services are available to schools but in some areas, particularly those where there are few bilingual pupils, external resources for schools may be scarce and, if parents want to be of assistance, this can be very helpful.

Working with parents in school

Some parents want to help in school, others may be invited to do so for a particular reason such as talking about a young baby or sharing a skill with the children. One-off visitors who come into class to share information or skills do much to enliven the curriculum and enthuse children. However, for such sessions to go well teachers need to liaise with the visitor to ensure that the content and presentation are appropriate. All visitors and volunteers need to know what they will be doing and why. Schools need to have procedures for briefing them. These may cover such things as:

- providing training for regular volunteers;
- giving visitors them specific tasks to do;
- providing explanations of how their visit contributes to the children's learning;
- ensuring that the children are prepared and understand the adult's role;
- preparing plans that identify what volunteers will be doing; and
- sharing expectations about behaviour and ways of working with children.

Home–school agreements

All schools have home–school agreements which were introduced in order to formalize the partnership between schools and homes. The agreement is intended to be a short document but it should set out the duties and responsibilities to each other of the school, parents and pupils. It might include how the school will teach and communicate information to pupils, how parents can contribute to their children's learning and success at school, and how children can contribute to their own learning and well-being in school. Some agreements stress rules and regulations such as good behaviour. However, the best agreements focus on learning and corresponding expectations for home, school and children are mirrored in each party's section, as in Figure 6.1. This reflects the shared interests of teachers, parents and children, and demonstrates a concern for partnership.

Parent–teacher meetings

Formally organized meetings between parents and teachers usually occur once a term. Very often these are early in the autumn term, as parents want to know how their child has settled into the new environment, and towards the end of the spring and summer terms. Parents may have received a written report prior to the meeting in the summer term and may wish to discuss this.

It is good practice to organize a range of times for the meetings during the day and in the evenings over the course of about a week. This gives parents the opportunity to attend even if they are working or have family commitments. Schools sometimes offer crèche facilities and again this can be helpful to parents with childcare responsibilities. The local educational authority can sometimes provide interpreters which is helpful for some parents.

There is often a great deal to discuss during the meeting. Teachers want to receive as well as give information, as do parents, so setting aside a reasonable length of time for each interview is sensible. Some schools have a policy of asking parents to let them know in advance if there are any particular issues that they want to raise so that teachers can prepare for these. Even if parents do not identify issues beforehand, they are likely to want to talk about their child's progress in communication, language and literacy. This is normally a priority so it is as well to prepare for this.

Activity

Only a few parents come to the teacher–parent interviews. Why might this be? We could assume that it is because they are not interested in their child's education or school. But you could also consider timing or childcare. If parents think that their child is not making very good progress, some might want to find out how they can best help their child but others might feel that their child's difficulties reflect badly on them and so stay away. What can be done to increase attendance?

Home–School Agreement

The school

The school will do its best to:

Ensure that your child enjoys and develops a positive attitude to learning

Provide a broad, balanced curriculum

Meet your child's needs

Keep you informed about your child's progress.

Parents/carers

I/We will do our best to:

Support my child's learning at home and at school

Support the school's policies

Provide information that will help the school to meet my child's needs

Discuss my child's progress with teachers.

Child

I will do my best to:

Learn at school

Enjoy learning

Take part in school life

Let adults know if I am unhappy or finding work difficult.

Signed....................(teacher) ....(parent) ....(child)

Figure 6.1 *Home–school agreement*

Working with teaching assistants, nursery assistants and learning support assistants

In the Foundation Stage it is common to have a number of differently qualified adults working together as a team. There may be nursery assistants, childcare assistants, learning support assistants, teaching assistants and other teachers.

Nursery assistants

Nursery assistants are important members of the teaching team in nursery and reception classes and other early years settings, and make a significant contribution to young children's education. As part of their training they learn about child development, health care, young children's learning and the organization and management of early years environments. They work with large and small groups of children as well as individuals, prepare materials and activities and contribute to planning and assessments of pupils. In day nurseries, which may be open for 10 or 12 hours each day, nursery assistants may also take care of young children's physical needs such as feeding, washing and sleep.

Learning support assistants

In the main, learning support assistants work with children who have special educational needs. They may support children so that they can access the curriculum that is offered to all children, or they may work on specially prepared activities that have been carefully matched to the child's needs. The teacher or lead practitioner and the learning support assistant work together closely to plan for children with special educational needs. They also share information about the child's changing needs, responses to activities and progress that they make. Individual support from a learning support assistant can in some cases lead to less involvement by the teacher, leaving the learning support assistant to deliver most of the curriculum. It is important that children receive attention from the teacher. It is also important that children do not rely excessively on the learning support assistant or one-to-one help to complete work. The aim is to help children, as far as possible, to move towards independent learning.

Teaching assistants

Teaching assistants are increasingly becoming highly qualified professionals and, like nursery assistants, they can make a significant contribution to teaching and learning. In recent years the Department for Education and Skills (DfES) has introduced a number of training programmes for teaching assistants, including higher-level courses which combine higher education and school-based training. Teaching assistants generally work with groups of children on activities that have been planned by the teacher. They may work with individuals or groups who need extra support. They can also undertake non-teaching duties such as putting up displays and photocopying which can give the teacher more time for teaching and planning.

In 2002 Ofsted published a best practice guide to the most effective deployment of teaching assistants. The findings were intended to provide a helpful starting point for planning the work of other adults in the literacy hour and so have particular application to reception classes which often benefit from a large share of a teaching assistant's time. Ofsted suggested that:

> In whole-class teaching, the teaching assistant helps pupils to learn better by:
> - minimizing distractions by dealing with individual pupils;
> - keeping individual pupils on task by prompting their responses;
> - repeating or rephrasing questions asked by the teacher;
> - providing additional or alternative explanations for individual pupils;
> - providing specialist support, for example for hearing-impaired pupils;
> - noting pupils' contributions so that the quieter pupils can receive extra attention later;
> - supporting less confident pupils, or those of lower ability or with SEN, to make contributions to the lesson.
>
> During group or independent work, the teaching assistant helps pupils to learn better through:
> - providing support for an individual or for a group of pupils which enables them to tackle tasks confidently that would otherwise seem too difficult for them;
> - giving more individual explanations of the task than is possible for the teacher to do with the whole class;
> - giving the teacher feedback about pupils' learning so that he or she can adjust later lessons;
> - giving pupils immediate and relevant feedback on their work. (Ofsted, 2002)

To make the best use of other adults in the classroom, teachers need to:

- have procedures for briefing support staff;
- be aware of assistants' capabilities;
- build in time to plan with assistants;
- plan for the best use of assistants' time;
- involve assistants in making assessments and sharing information; and
- support them in developing professional skills.

Non-teaching colleagues

In addition to parents and practitioners, staff in the Foundation Stage will work with other non-teaching colleagues such as caretakers, school secretaries and mid-day supervisors. They can sometimes offer different perspectives on children's abilities. For example, children who appear quiet in the classroom may be confident and articulate when with their friends at lunchtime. Children who seem to lack the motor skills needed to hold writing implements and produce controlled handwriting may be able to write more fluently in the relaxed environment of an after school club.

Support staff

School secretaries, caretakers and mid-day supervisors can all contribute to the well-being of children when they are at school. Staff who are concerned with the maintenance of the buildings can play a part in ensuring that equipment and the environment are safe. Discussion can lead to a solution about problems with health and safety issues or provide ideas about how to make effective use of resources and the school grounds. Mid-day supervisors can play a part in settling new children into the nursery or school and help them to make friends.

Playworkers

Playworkers receive training that enables them to work in breakfast clubs, after-school clubs and holiday playschemes. They work with children on a range of activities including sports, art and craft, music and play opportunities. They help to provide safe spaces for children to play and learn before and after the normal school day. Playworkers usually organize and run activities without the direct involvement of teachers but they often use school premises. Their work with children means that they get to know children in a different context to teachers and, so, exchanging information can be beneficial.

School library services

Librarians who work with schools have a great deal of knowledge about books, reading and the curriculum requirements for young children. They are available to work with schools and can provide a number of services varying from helping to update and restock existing school libraries, to running storytelling workshops for teachers, parents and children or lending boxes of books carefully selected to cater for particular age groups and topics. Children's librarians also run special events for children in school holidays, and schools can publicize these to parents.

Working with other agencies

Practitioners in the Foundation Stage have always worked with other agencies particularly those concerned with the health and welfare of children. One of the intentions behind *Every Child Matters* (DfES, 2004a) is to improve information-sharing and partnership between a variety of services which are concerned with children, in order to provide for the needs of children and their families. Before admission and subsequently throughout the year, other professionals may be involved formally or informally with the child and family. These professionals may include a health visitor, an educational psychologist, a speech and language therapist, and an occupational therapist. In working with other professionals an ethos of mutual trust and openness is essential, as is respect for the range of skills and expertise that each contributes to a coordinated service for children and their families. At the heart of inter-professional collaboration is the need for early identification and assessment, which can be used to develop an appropriate individual educational programme for each child.

Most health-related difficulties are recognized by parents or carers outside school, but sometimes teachers notice potential problems and might want to discuss these with health professionals when they visit to conduct medical examinations and screen children for potential problems such as hearing loss. School staff may need to liaise and exchange information with speech therapists and educational psychologists about the special educational needs of some pupils. Teachers will need to find time for discussions with regular visitors, such as teachers who support children who are learning English as an additional language, in order to exchange information and plan a suitable programme of work.

Activity

Finding time for the Foundation Stage team to meet to share observations of children, ideas about planning and to allocate adults to activities can be difficult. Do you know which times suit all the members of the staff team? Can you find a good time for everyone to meet? Do you have a clear idea about what needs to be discussed?

Conclusion

Each of the many diverse settings which provide education in the early years is a community consisting of professionals, parents and children. When all these groups communicate, share information and work together, children benefit. One of the key roles of the early years educational professional is to ensure that all the adults in the setting use their skills for the good of children.

 Further reading

Hornby, G. (2000) *Improving Parental Involvement*. London: Cassell.
This provides a good general introduction to all aspects of parental involvement.

Wolfendale, S. and Bastiani, J. (eds) (2000) *The Contribution of Parents to School Effectiveness*. London: David Fulton.
This book contains chapters describing some recent initiatives in parental involvement. It also explores some of the issues that practitioners need to address.

Chapter 7

Assessment

Introduction

Most early years practitioners spend a great deal of time assessing children. They do this because they want to make sure that children are progressing, they need to identify any special needs that children have, they want to gauge the effectiveness of their teaching, they need to report to parents and other practitioners about children's learning and they need to complete formal assessments at the end of the Foundation Stage. They spend their time:

- gathering information;
- recording information; and
- acting on assessment information.

This chapter examines what should be assessed in communication, language and literacy. In it I describe different types of assessment and how to gather and record evidence for assessment from pupils, parents and adults who work with children. There are suggestions about how to integrate assessment into teaching through planning. The final part of the chapter looks at reporting to parents and other practitioners.

Types of assessment

We are all very aware that there are two main forms of assessment:

- summative, and
- formative.

Summative assessment

Summative assessment summarizes where learners are at a given point in time. It is usually completed at the end of a period of learning, such as at the end of a term or a year, and provides a summary of what has been learned. It is also known as assessment of learning. The Foundation Stage Profile (QCA, 2003) which is completed towards the end of the Foundation Stage is an example of such a summary. Information from summative assessment can be used to make adjustments to medium- or long-term plans, to highlight areas of weakness in teaching and to set curricular targets for the setting.

Summative assessment does not usually tell us about how children learn, their attitudes to learning or their understanding. It tends to measure skills such as

- can write his or her name;
- knows that print goes from left to right; and
- forms recognizable letters.

These skills are part of leaning to be literate and need to be taught. So, if we discover that children cannot do them, opportunities to practise them will have to be planned. However, they are not the only things that need to be assessed. Practitioners need to know such things as:

- Do children enjoy reading and writing?
- What sorts of books do they enjoy?
- Do children see writing as having some relevance to their lives?
- When do children talk confidently?
- What is the quality of the children's written and spoken ideas?
- What would individual children like to be able to do better?

Summative assessment provides an overview of what children can do and provides general pointers about the nature of the provision. For example, if a number of children cannot write their names by the end of nursery then maybe there are not enough opportunities for them to do this, so the provision may have to be extended. However, summative assessment cannot tell us how to improve the quality of the learning experiences. For example, children might be given opportunities to copy their names from name cards once a week but if they still cannot write their names on their paintings, labels or in pieces of writing, they are not able to transfer their skill to other situations. So we need to know, do the children see the point of the name-copying activity and do they understand the use of labelling items with their name? The answers to these questions help us to provide children with meaningful learning experiences and help improve the quality of the provision. Summative assessments do not tell us about children's attitudes or dispositions to their learning. Do they engage with activities enthusiastically? Are they curious, willing to explore and take risks? Or are they passive, eager to finish adult-led activities and fearful of making mistakes? Again the answers to these questions help us to provide for the individual needs of children and may cause us to reflect on and change the nature of the experiences we provide for them.

Formative assessment

Formative assessment should enable us to find out not just about the products of learning, but also about the processes of learning. It is sometimes called assessment for learning and it is ongoing. Formative assessment occurs as children are working and during the daily activities in the classroom, and is embedded in planning and teaching. It helps practitioners to recognize what children can do or any particular difficulties that individuals might be having. It can give us information about what children know, how they learn and their attitudes towards learning. This enables practitioners to plan the next steps for learning that will help children progress in their learning in the short or medium term. Information from formative assessments is used to:

- provide relevant feedback to learners;
- adjust teaching to take account of what has been discovered through assessment;
- provide meaningful learning opportunities; and
- meet individual learning needs.

Collecting assessment information

Information for both summative and formative assessments can be collected in the same ways. However, there are short cuts to collecting information for summative assessments. Observations can be used to complete checklists which are filled in with ticks or crosses but without any information about the depth of the child's understanding. Listening to children reading can be undertaken with a view to identifying if the child can recognize high-frequency words or use phonic skills when decoding, but information about the child's understanding of the text or their feelings about particular types of books, authors or illustrators may not be gathered or recorded.

Collecting information about children's learning can be done in a number of ways. The most effective are an integral part of the daily routine and focus on everyday activities. Much of the information can be used to benefit children's learning in the short term by informing the daily and weekly planning. If appropriate, information gathered in this way can be transferred to records of summative assessments. The main methods of collecting assessment information in the Foundation Stage are through:

- observing;
- talking to children;
- analysing samples of work;
- pupil self-assessment;
- collecting information from parents; and
- testing.

Observing

Most effective observations are planned, but it is also possible to gain valuable information from incidental observations. Observations that are planned need to have an identified focus, which can be a child, an activity or an area of learning. The time, the person who is doing the observation and the method of recording the information need to be identified ahead of the observation. Planned observations are often identified on the short-term plan when practitioners have seen which activities are likely to provide valuable assessment information. The focus of the observations may be the learning objectives for the activity as well as the way children undertake the activity, their understanding and their engagement. There should be a planned rolling programme of observations which ensure that over the course of a term all the children have been observed in a range of contexts for each aspect of each area of learning. Teacher-initiated activities, child-initiated activities, independent activities, group activities, work and play can all be observed.

Unplanned observations occur during the course of the adults' normal monitoring of activities and work with the children. Sometimes one hears or sees something striking which reveals something new or unexpected about what a child knows or understands. A child who generally plays alone or with one special friend might be observed joining in an activity with a different group of children. This new behaviour might indicate the child's growing confidence in talking to others. Two children might be noticed playing with the story props in the listening area and incorporating language from the story into their retelling. One of these children might never previously have chosen to look at books or seemed very interested in stories, and so this might indicate a new direction in the child's learning. Surprising new information which has been identified through incidental observations might be followed up with planned observations which will enable the teacher to investigate what was seen and allow additional information to be gathered.

Sometimes when looking back on a series of observations, practitioners realize that some children have not been observed at all. Such children might be quiet, well behaved or have been absent. It can be a good idea to undertake a timed observation of such children perhaps for three two-minute slots over a 30-minute period. This can reveal the choices that the children make, how involved they are with their work or who they choose to work with. This could be followed up with a conversation with the child to gather more information.

Talking to children

Talking to children about their learning is valuable in its own right, as articulating ideas can deepen children's understanding of what has been learned and shows them that learning is valued. It also provides information about children's understanding that might not be apparent by just observing what children do. Children are able to tell us what they find easy or difficult and what they would like to learn. Their ideas can make a contribution to the planning of future work that will interest them and help them achieve things that are important to them.

As well as having conversations with children, adults can question children about their learning. Open-ended questions such as 'What do you think about ... ?' or 'Why do you think ... ?' or 'Is there another way ... ?' can help us assess children's understanding as well as sometimes taking their learning further. Questions should be used sparingly and as part of natural conversations with children. If they are not, we run the risk of children becoming exasperated with adults and revealing very little, as the following response from a rather frustrated child shows: 'Why do you keep asking the kids questions when you knows all the answers? Like ... what colour is it then? You can see for yourself it's red ... so why do you keep asking them?' (Cousins, 1990: 30).

Whatever the context, children should participate fully in conversations and should do much of the talking, and adults should genuinely want to find out about the children and their pursuits. Talking to children can help us to find out:

- what interests children;
- what motivates children to want to learn;
- how children perceive themselves as learners;
- what children already know and can do;
- what children would like to be able to know about and do;
- how children have approached an activity;
- what they have found interesting; and
- where their misunderstandings might be.

Opportunities to talk with children may need to be planned. Certainly time will need to be allocated to talking with individuals and joining in with their play and their work. Always teaching large and small groups may not allow us to determine what has been learned.

Activity

Think about the sort of language you could use when you want to talk to children to find out about their understanding, their attitude to learning and what they would like to learn.

Analysing samples of work

Anything that is written or made can be analysed to discover what children know and understand. Sometimes the child's work, such as a piece of writing, a drawing or a model, can provide the stimulus for a discussion and the child's words can be used to annotate the work. In communication, language and literacy it is common to discuss recorded work with the child, and in doing so assess what the child has done, comment on the strengths and provide advice on how to improve. Although reading is not recorded in the same way, a child's reading is a sample of work and adults can learn a great deal about a child's reading ability by listening attentively, making notes about strengths and difficulties, and talking to children about their reading and books.

A drawing sample
The drawing in Figure 7.1 was produced by a 4-year-old girl, Sophie, in a reception class. It shows Sophie, her sisters and her mum having dinner in

Pizza Hut. As Sophie talked about her drawing she produced an oral recount of this event, covering all the when, where, who and why elements of a recount text. She included some detail about the type of meal that each person chose and how her mum and her youngest sister had shared a pizza. The outing had been arranged to mark one of her sisters' birthday, hence the candles at the end of the table. They had all dressed up for the occasion, mum had put beads in the girls' hair and had herself worn a pair of long dangly ear rings. In this discussion with the adult, Sophie showed a firm grasp of narrative. She gave her recount a title, *It's about going to Pizza Hut*, an opening, *At the weekend we went to Pizza Hut*, an ending, *We all ate everything up, Silver was tired, she cried, and mum said time to go*, and was able to structure the telling around a series of events related in sequence. This opportunity to discuss her drawing showed that Sophie could use oral language to communicate and engage an audience. It also showed that Sophie has the skills needed to recount a factual event and to create a narrative. These skills will feed in directly to any writing that Sophie produces.

Figure 7.1 *A drawing sample*

A writing sample

Figure 7.2 is a piece of unaided writing by Adam, a 4-year-old boy in a nursery class. He told the practitioner that he was writing and drawing all about himself. He spoke with pleasure and confidence about his ability to write and draw detailed pictures now that he was 4. He said that he knew about 'big' letters and 'little' letters and how he preferred to use 'big' letters for his name. When he was asked if he had included the word *look* in order to signal to readers of his work that they look at the writing or look at the picture, Adam replied that he included this because he knew how to read and write the word and he had also seen the *oo* drawn like eyes. He went on to talk about his picture, pointing to different parts of his body and describing his hair, his eyes and his belly.

Figure 7.2 *A writing sample*

Just looking at this piece of writing suggests that Adam knows a great deal about writing but talking to him revealed the pride and confidence Adam had in his own ability and that he was aware of writing in the environment perhaps showing his interest in writing and his eye for detail. Noticing that Adam used his picture to give information additional to his writing, the practitioner thought that Adam and other children in the class might enjoy some drawing and labelling activities as this would bring together their interest in writing and drawing. This would stretch them a little further and give them the opportunity to experiment with a different type of writing. The conversation with Adam and the analysis of his writing and his drawing had given her information about Adam and helped to inform future planning for him and for the nursery.

A reading sample

Jo was a 4-year-old boy in a nursery class. He often chose to look at familiar books in the reading area. One morning the practitioner observed Jo as he selected *Red Rockets and Rainbow Jelly* (Heap and Sharratt, 2004). He pored over the pages and was reading the pictures and retelling the text in his own words. Not wanting to disturb Jo's enjoyment, the teacher made a note of the confident way that Jo was interacting with the book and planned an opportunity to share the book together. A few days later, seeing Jo in the reading area, the teacher joined him and selected *Red Rockets and Rainbow Jelly* to look at herself. Jo said that he liked the book and the teacher invited him to read it with her. This he did. Jo's reading and comments are contained in the speech bubbles in Figure 7.3.

What Jo knows about reading   This was an accomplished and sustained retelling of the book which was faithful to the authors' intentions and showed understanding of what had been written. Jo used the illustrations to support his reading and these played a large part in his success. Where the illustrations are simplest, his retelling is closest to the actual text; where they contain more detail, he is likely just to talk about the part of the illustration that he finds most interesting. However, this is more than a retelling using the illustrations as prompts. Jo has remembered the names of the characters and can identify these as the key protagonists in the book. He realizes the book is about them. He is also able to use story language as he produces complete sentences containing sentence structures similar to those often used in children's picture books. He follows the *I like* format for much of the reading generally, deviating from this when the illustrations suggest that the text might be saying something else. For example, the illustration accompanying the sentence 'Sue likes everything blue' shows Sue sitting on a beach surrounded by toys that one might take to the seaside. As Jo read, he often moved his finger along the line of print in the text and showed his awareness of the direction and placement of text when he commented on the unusual arrangement of the words around the picture of the jelly. Jo was also able to bring his own experience of the world to his reading as he commented about not liking pears and having a cat as a pet. He realized that, like a character in a book, he has a story of his own. He is able to compare his own experiences and preferences with those expressed by the characters in the book.

Assessing Jo's reading   In this reading there is evidence that Jo is making very good progress towards becoming a reader. He wants to read and is highly motivated. He has some favourite books, authors and illustrators. He finds reading stories pleasurable and recognizes that books can reflect or add to

Jo reading *Red Rockets and Rainbow Jelly* by Sue Heap and Nick Sharratt

This is Nick.

This is Sue.

> This is Nick. This is Sue.

Nick likes red apples.

Sue likes green pears.

> Nick likes apples. Sue likes pears. I don't.

Nick likes yellow socks.

Sue likes yellow ducks.

> Nick has some socks. Sue likes ducks.

Nick likes orange hair.

Sue likes purple hair …

And purple flowers.

> Nick has red hair, like a wig. Sue has curly hair. It's purple.

Nick likes brown bears and black cats.

> Nick likes bears and cats.

Sue likes black and white cats and black and white hats.

> Sue likes cats. I've got a cat too.

Nick likes red cars.

Sue likes pink and orange cars.

> Nick is in a car. Sue's got a car.

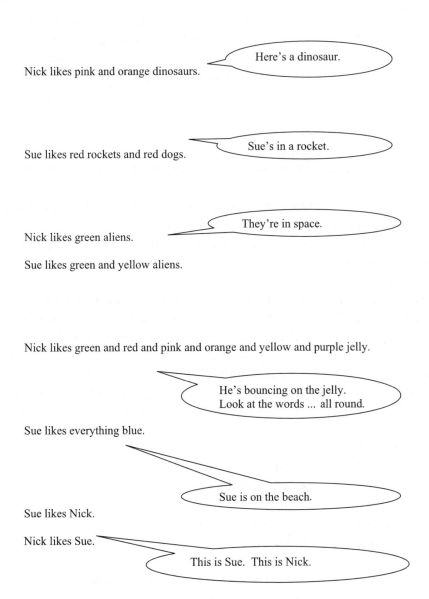

Nick likes pink and orange dinosaurs.   *Here's a dinosaur.*

Sue likes red rockets and red dogs.   *Sue's in a rocket.*

Nick likes green aliens.   *They're in space.*

Sue likes green and yellow aliens.

Nick likes green and red and pink and orange and yellow and purple jelly.

He's bouncing on the jelly.
Look at the words ... all round.

Sue likes everything blue.

Sue is on the beach.

Sue likes Nick.

Nick likes Sue.

This is Sue. This is Nick.

Figure 7.3 *A reading sample*

the reader's experiences. He understands what he reads. He is developing a number of reading strategies including word recognition and use of context. He has a sense of the completeness of book language. In this reading Jo demonstrates that he has met six of the nine points on the assessment scales for reading in the Foundation Stage Profile (QCA, 2003). He:

- is developing an interest in books;
- knows that print conveys meaning;
- recognizes a few familiar words;
- knows that in English, print is read from left to right and top to bottom;
- shows an understanding of the elements of stories, such as main character, sequence of events and openings; and
- retells narratives in the correct sequence, drawing on the language patterns of stories.

Using assessment information to help children progress   The value of making assessments of pupils' learning is that one can plan learning experiences that will help them to make further progress. Jo's interest and ability in reading suggest that the next step for him is to begin to recognize some frequently used words when he is reading, whilst continuing to develop his confidence and maintain his enjoyment of reading. He needs lots of opportunities to see and remember key words. Activities that will help him to do both might include:

- continuing to read and reread books that are familiar;
- sharing familiar books with adults;
- listening to books on tape;
- reading more simple books by Nick Sharratt;
- shared reading of core books;
- discussing books and stories;
- making up his own stories based on known texts; and
- games such as word bingo, snap and book-based games.

Activity

Read through the example of Mollie's reading in Chapter 3 and try to set a target for her reading development to be achieved by the end of the term. Suggest some activities which will help her to reach her target.

Activity

Analyse a sample of reading gathered when you are sharing a book with a child or when the child is joining in with the reading or the child is attempting to read unaided. What can you learn about the child's attitudes to reading and his or her use of reading strategies? What might be the next steps for this child and how would you provide for them?

Pupil self-assessment

Even the youngest children can start to reflect on their own learning. Nurseries which follow a plan do review approach, make time each day for children to think and talk about the activities that they have done and consider what they might do in the future. School-made individual books which contain photographs of the child engaged in different activities can be used as a prompt for teachers and children to reflect on what has been done and learned, and to reflect on learning over the course of a term or a year. These are also a good way of showing parents what children do when they are at school. Children can select pieces of work and photographs to include in their portfolios. The reasons for their choices can be dictated by the child and written down by the practitioner.

In reception classes children can be introduced to a more detailed form of self-assessment in which they assess their work and understanding against learning objectives. This can be introduced during guided reading or guided writing sessions. Plenary sessions are an ideal opportunity for children to review their own work and that of others. A group of children can report on their work, and the rest of the class can offer advice on how to improve the work as well as give praise for what has been achieved. Over the longer term children can be asked to review the progress they have made during a term and the year. They can write their own reports, which will be sent home with the teacher's report. The children's report can be discussed and used as a way for the teacher and the child to set targets for the next term.

Collecting information from parents

Parents have a great deal of information about their children, and this can be shared with practitioners and added to records of assessments. They can tell us about their child's particular skills and interests. Some children who are rather quiet at school may be talkative at home; others may not read very much at school but read comics, magazines and information books at home. This kind of information helps to build up a more rounded picture of the child's achievements as well as providing information that can be used to make the curriculum relevant to them.

Parents can share information during visits and interviews prior to their children starting in the nursery or reception class, during teacher–parent conferences which often happen each term, through home–school diaries, at the start and end of each day or through individual appointments. Practitioners have to give parents a written report about their child once every year and this is usually discussed with parents. The Foundation Stage Profile has space for parents' comments which should be taken into account when making judgements about children's progress.

Testing

Testing means short recall sessions such as letter recognition activities carried out for a brief period before lunch or play times, or writing spellings on a whiteboard at the end of a literacy session. Quick review checks where children are asked to remember important aspects of some previous learning such as the events from a story can be carried out at the start of a session. The children's responses to these quick tests help practitioners to identify any children who might need further practice or re-teaching. They do provide assessment opportunities, but they do not provide the same breadth and quality of information as that offered by the other methods outlined in this section.

Recording assessment information

Assessments need to be recorded but systems for doing this need to be manageable as record-keeping can take up significant lengths of time. It is common but not obligatory for nurseries and reception classes to have assessment portfolios for each child. At the start these will contain information from parents, and in the case of a child entering with an already identified special need, information from other agencies. Gradually, as the staff learn more about the child, additional information such as observations, photographs, samples of work, pupils' self-assessments and reports will be added during the Foundation Stage. All entries should be dated and annotated to show their significance.

Observations can be made in notebooks, on sticky notes or on activity sheets. Some practitioners have activity sheets as in Figure 7.4. These are filled in after a group of children have finished an adult-led activity. It helps teachers to keep track of the children who have completed an activity as well as showing the level of each child's understanding.

Story maps 25.04.06	Learning objective Reading Yellow: Begin to be aware of the way stories are structured	Learning objective Reading Grey: Retell narratives in the correct sequence, drawing on language pattern of stories
Charlie Simpson		Keen to get the sequence in the correct order Checked with book
Sadie Malcolm	Set up a farm rather than re-telling story	
Tammy Marsh		Said, 'Rosie the hen went for a walk…'
Francis Okiri	Felt sorry for the fox compared him to the wolf in 'Suddenly'	

Figure 7.4 *Activity sheet*

Any notes that are made can be kept as they are and placed in a general assessment folder, or significant information can be transferred to an individual checklist such as that in Figure 7.5 which has been designed to record progress in language for communication and language for thinking. In Figure 7.5 the column on the left lists the stepping stones and Early Learning Goals. The column on the right can be used to make notes on the child's achievements, including dates, activities and significant things that are said. Checklists are kept in individual children's portfolios.

At the end of each term the contents of the portfolio can be checked and the information used to complete part of the Foundation Stage Profile (QCA, 2003). Doing this provides practitioners with a summary of the children's progress to date and helps them to check that they are gaining a broad picture of each child and assessing all that will be required to complete the profile at the end of the reception year.

Language for communication	Name
	Notes
Interact with others	
Use words and/or gestures, including body language such as eye contact and facial expression, to communicate	
Use simple statements and questions often linked to gestures	
Use intonation, rhythm and phrasing to make their meaning clear to others	
Have emerging self-confidence to speak to others about wants and interests	
Use simple grammatical structures	
Ask simple questions, often in the form of 'where' or 'what'	
Talk alongside others, rather than with them. Use talk to gain attention and initiate exchanges. Use action rather than talk to demonstrate or explain to others	
Initiate conversation, attend to and take account of what others say, and use talk to resolve disagreements	
Interact with others, negotiating plans and activities and taking turns in conversation	
Listening	
Listen to favourite nursery rhymes, stories and songs. Join in with repeated refrains, anticipating key events and important phrases	
Respond to simple instructions	
Listen to others in one-to-one/small groups when conversation interests them	
Listen to stories with increasing attention and recall	
Describe main story settings, events and principal characters	
Question why things happen, and give explanations	
Initiate a conversation, negotiate positions, pay attention to and take account of others' views	

Figure 7.5 *Checklist of progress in language for communication and language for thinking*

Enjoy listening to and using spoken and written language, and readily turn to it in their play and learning	
Sustain attentive listening, responding to what they have heard by relevant comments, questions or actions	
Listen with enjoyment, and respond to stories, songs and other music, rhymes and poems and make up their own stories, songs, rhymes and poems	
Vocabulary	
Use familiar words, often in isolation, to identify what they do and do not want	
Use vocabulary focused on objects and people who are of particular importance to them	
Build up vocabulary that reflects the breadth of their experiences	
Begin to experiment with language describing possession	
Extend vocabulary, especially by grouping and naming	
Use vocabulary and forms of speech that are increasingly influenced by experience of books	
Extend their vocabulary, exploring the meanings and sounds of new words	
Speaking	
Use isolated words and phrases and/or gestures to communicate with those well known to them	
Begin to use more complex sentences	
Use a widening range of words to express or elaborate ideas	
Link statements and stick to a main theme or intention	
Consistently develop a simple story, explanation or line of questioning	
Use language for an increasing range of purposes	
Confidently talk to people other than those who are well known to them	

continues over page

Speak clearly and audibly with confidence and control and show awareness of the listener, for example by their use of conventions such as greetings, 'please' and 'thank you'	
Language for thinking	
Use action, sometimes with limited talk, that is largely concerned with the 'here and now'	
Talk activities through, reflecting on and modifying what they are doing	
Use talk to give new meanings to objects and actions, treating them as symbols for other things	
Use talk to connect ideas, explain what is happening and anticipate what might happen next	
Use talk, actions and objects to recall and relive past experiences	
Begin to use talk instead of action to rehearse, reorder and reflect on past experience, linking significant events from own experience and from stories, paying attention to sequence and how events lead into one another	
Begin to make patterns in their experience through linking cause and effect, sequencing, ordering and grouping	
Begin to use talk to pretend imaginary situations	
Use language to imagine and recreate roles and experiences	
Use talk to organize, sequence and clarify thinking, ideas, feelings and events	

Using assessment information

Information from assessments can sometimes be used immediately to give oral and written feedback to children. It can also be used to adjust planning and teaching for the next day, week or theme.

Feedback

Immediate oral feedback to the children can be one of the most powerful ways of teaching children. Black and William (1998), in an extensive review of research and writing about assessment, found that oral feedback is more effective than written feedback and it is a key factor in improving learning. It relates to the child's immediate needs and is given while the products and processes of activities are fresh in the child's mind. The teacher's comments usually follow a discussion with the child, but the response can be mixed with requests for more information. Cambourne (1988: 61) called these 'instructional conversations' and identified the benefits as, 'The teacher … can gain insights into what [children] know and how they are thinking. The children … develop their competence and fine tune their knowledge by using the teacher's competence and consciousness to complement their own.'

Writing is often something that teachers and children discuss together. When responding to children's early writing, practitioners do at least some of the following:

- respond with respect to what the child has produced;
- ask the child to read back or talk about what they have written;
- talk about the content;
- comment on significant aspects of transcription;
- write the correct version;
- write a comment, a question, a reply;
- select one teaching point to discuss or demonstrate; and
- display, use or show the child their writing is valued.

In the example of Adam's writing (Figure 7.2) the practitioner could have given many different types of feedback to him had she judged that it was appropriate to do so. After commenting positively on what he had written, she could have:

- talked about how it is customary to use lower case letters in one's name, apart from the first letter, and looked at examples of how names are written;
- shown him how to label his picture with words such as, *eyes* and *hair*;
- written a response such as *I can see Adam and he has got big eyes*;
- written a question for him to answer in writing such as, *What colour are your eyes?* and
- shown him how to form a lower case *a*.

Any of these would have contributed to Adam's growing understanding of writing and how to write.

If the writing has been produced with a learning objective in mind such as 'to write labels and captions for pictures and drawings' (DfES, 2001a), a text-level objective for children in the reception year, it is important to consider whether the child has met the objective. Has the child written single words or phrases as labels or have they produced complete sentences which would be inappropriate? Have they understood the concept of a label or will they need more practice at this? If it has not been understood, then some direct teaching can happen immediately and the learning objective may need to be revisited in a future session.

Activity

Make a list of the sorts of things you could say to children or ask them to begin an episode of giving oral feedback. Think about being positive, focusing on the learning intentions, using open questions and helping children to move on.

Activity

Look at some samples of writing produced by young children. How would you respond orally and in writing? What would be your immediate teaching point for each of the children?

Planning and teaching

The value of assessment information is the impact it can have on children's future learning. For this to happen, assessment notes have to be analysed to see what children were able to do or understand. Then decisions can be made about future teaching and the next steps in children's learning can be planned for. What has been learned about the children may lead practitioners to adapt the planned work for later in the week or it could be taken into account in the next week's work. For example, in the notes made on the activity sheet in Figure 7.4 the practitioner observed that two children did not seem to recognize or be able to articulate the structure of stories. They would probably have benefited from extra practice at retelling stories and identifying significant events. To give them this practice she might have planned further activities using different resources such as sequencing cards or story props.

Summative assessments at the end of a year might feed into the long- and medium-term plans for the Foundation Stage. If the summative assessments reveal that a number of children have a weakness in the same aspect of an area of learning, practitioners may decide to prioritize that curriculum area next year. They will need to consider if the provision could be improved in some way. Such information might have significance for the Year 1 teachers who are receiving the children, as they too might need to prioritize an aspect of learning that many children have found difficult.

The Foundation Stage Profile

The Foundation Stage Profile (QCA, 2003) is a way of summing up practitioners' assessments of children which have occurred during the Foundation Stage. Although it should be completed at the end of the reception year, it is organized in a way that allows entries to be made throughout the Foundation Stage.

The profile consists of a set of 13 assessment scales covering the six areas of learning. Each assessment scale is linked to one or more aspects of learning and has nine points. For communication, language and literacy there are four assessment scales: language for communication and thinking, linking sounds and letters, reading and writing. In each scale the first three points are based on the stepping stones in the *Curriculum Guidance for the Foundation Stage* (QCA, 2000b), the next five on the Early Learning Goals, and the final point describes children who are working consistently beyond the level of the Early Learning Goals. Each point is ticked as it is securely achieved.

There is space in the profile for contributions from children, parents and additional information perhaps from the child's records in a previous setting. The Foundation Stage Profile forms the basis for reports to parents and for information that can be passed on to the child's next teacher. It can be used instead of a conventional written report and should be discussed with parents.

Assessing bilingual pupils

The assessments in the Foundation Stage Profile (QCA, 2003) address three aspects of the achievements of bilingual children. These are:

- development in the home language;
- development across the curriculum assessed through the home language; and
- development of English.

Development in the home language

Practitioners need to find out as much as possible about the home language or languages of young learners who are acquiring English as an additional language. Parents and carers, bilingual support teachers or previous practitioners may be able to provide information. For each bilingual child the practitioner might want to find out:

- Which language(s) does the child understand?
- Which language(s) does the child speak?

- Does he or she always use the same language with particular adults or children? (For example, a child may speak the home language to parents or grandparents but speak English to brothers and sisters.)
- What language experiences does the child have in the home language? Does he or she know rhymes, poems or stories?
- Are there any plans for the child to learn to read and write in the home language?
- How does the child's language development compare with that of any siblings?

Answers to these questions will help practitioners to provide appropriate experiences within the early years setting. They will also help to identify whether the child has any language delay or disorder, or other special needs, in addition to learning English. In order to monitor the progress children make in developing their home language, practitioners will probably depend on information from parents and siblings, EAL teachers and the child.

Development of English

Children who begin the Foundation Stage as learners of English as an additional language will progress in English at different rates to their monolingual peers. The QCA (2000a) assessment scales for assessing English as an additional language provide a useful way of assessing children's English language ability on entry to the Foundation Stage and monitoring the progress that they make thereafter. These are reproduced in Figure 7.6. The scales show the steps that children will take in speaking and listening, reading and writing as they move towards and through level 1 of the National Curriculum.

The extended scale for listening

Step 1 Pupils listen attentively for short bursts of time. They use non-verbal gestures to respond to greetings and questions about themselves, and they follow simple instructions based on the routines of the classroom.

Step 2 Pupils understand simple conversational English. They listen and respond to the gist of general explanations by the teacher where language is supported by non-verbal cues, including illustrations.

Level 1 (Threshold) With support, pupils understand and respond appropriately to straightforward comments or instructions addressed to them. They listen attentively to a range of speakers, including teacher presentation to the whole class.

Level 1 (Secure) In familiar contexts, pupils follow what others say about what they are doing and thinking. They listen with understanding to sequences of instructions and usually respond appropriately in conversation.

The extended scale for speaking

Step 1 Pupils echo words and expressions drawn from classroom routines and social interactions to communicate meaning. They express some basic needs, using single words or phrases in English.

Step 2 Pupils copy talk that has been modelled. In their speech, they show some control of English word order and their pronunciation is generally intelligible.

Level 1 (Threshold) Pupils speak about matters of immediate interest in familiar settings. They convey meaning through talk and gesture and can extend what they say with support. Their speech is sometimes grammatically incomplete at word and phrase level.

Level 1 (Secure) Pupils speak about matters of interest to a range of listeners and begin to develop connected utterances. What they say shows some grammatical complexity in expressing relationships between ideas and sequences of events. Pupils convey meaning, sustaining their contributions and the listeners' interest.

The extended scale for reading

Step 1 Pupils participate in reading activities. They know that, in English, print is read from left to right and from top to bottom. They recognize their names and familiar words and identify some letters of the alphabet by shape and sound.

Step 2 Pupils begin to associate sounds with letters in English and to predict what the text will be about. They read words and phrases that they have learned in different curriculum areas. With support, they can follow a text read aloud.

Level 1 (Threshold) Pupils can read a range of familiar words, and identify initial and final sounds in unfamiliar words. With support, they can establish meaning when reading aloud phrases or simple sentences, and use contextual clues to gain understanding. They respond to events and ideas in poems, stories and non-fiction.

Level 1 (Secure) Pupils use their knowledge of letters, sounds and words to establish meaning when reading familiar texts aloud, sometimes with prompting. They comment on events or ideas in poems, stories and non-fiction.

The extended scale for writing

Step 1 Pupils use English letters and letter-like forms to convey meaning. They copy or write their names and familiar words, and write from left to right.

Step 2 Pupils attempt to express meanings in writing, supported by oral work or pictures. Generally their writing is intelligible to themselves and a familiar reader, and shows some knowledge of sound and letter patterns in English spelling. Building on their knowledge of literacy in another language, pupils show knowledge of the function of sentence division.

Level 1 (Threshold) Pupils produce recognizable letters and words in texts, which convey meaning and show some knowledge of English sentence division and word order. Most commonly used letters are correctly shaped, but may be inconsistent in their size and orientation.

Level 1 (Secure) Pupils use phrases and longer statements which convey ideas to the reader, making some use of full stops and capital letters. Some grammatical patterns are irregular and pupils' grasp of English sounds and how they are written is not secure. Letters are usually clearly shaped and correctly orientated.

Figure 7.6 *The QCA guidance and assessment scales*

Reporting assessment information to parents

Parents are legally entitled to receive a report on their child's progress at the end of the Foundation Stage. This may be the Foundation Stage Profile (QCA, 2003). In addition most parents of children in nursery settings will also receive an end-of-year report. Written reports are complemented by termly meetings when parents and teachers can discuss children's progress and exchange information.

Many Foundation Stage settings have a system of open portfolios which are available for parents to read. These give parents a great deal of information about the activities available to children and the progress they are making in their learning. Parents can add comments to the portfolio or talk to practitioners about its contents and their own perceptions of their child's learning at home. This gives staff access to information that they might not otherwise have and which can be added to their records.

Conclusion

Assessment is a key part of planning and teaching. Undertaken well it enables practitioners to become informed about children's learning and the progress they are making, monitor the quality and appropriateness of planning and teaching, and match the curriculum to the interests and learning needs of children.

 Further reading

Clarke, S. (2003) *Enriching Feedback in the Primary Classroom: Oral and Written Feedback from Teachers and Children.* London: Hodder & Stoughton.
Although this book is chiefly aimed at those working in Key Stages 1 and 2, it contains examples taken from reception age children and many of the approaches to assessment are applicable to very young children.

Qualifications and Curriculum Authority (QCA) (2000) *A Language in Common: Assessing English as an Additional Language.* London: QCA.
This provides information about monitoring and assessing progress in learning English along with exemplification material.

Qualifications and Curriculum Authority (QCA) (2003) *Foundation Stage Profile Handbook.* London: QCA.
This publication gives detailed guidance on completing the Foundation Stage Profile as well as suggestions about assessment in the Foundation Stage.

Chapter 8

Planning for communication, language and literacy

Introduction

This chapter describes long-, medium- and short-term planning in the nursery and in reception classes. It includes suggestions about how to plan an inclusive curriculum and how to plan for progression by using assessment information. The chapter contains a number of sample plans that reflect the different ways of planning in the early and later parts of the Foundation Stage. All the examples show how teaching and learning communication, language and literacy can be located in a play-based curriculum and one that is relevant to young children.

Reasons for planning

Careful planning is the essential precursor to effective teaching and productive and enjoyable learning, it 'is the key to making children's learning effective, exciting, varied and progressive' (QCA, 2001: 2). It ensures that children in the Foundation Stage will have learning experiences that:

- cover all six areas of learning;
- cover all aspects of each area of learning in a balanced way;
- help to make learning coherent by linking different areas of learning;
- are varied rather than repetitive;
- help to consolidate and build on earlier learning;
- help them to make progress;
- match their learning needs; and
- result in tangible and satisfying outcomes.

Types of plans

Different settings and schools often devise their own planning systems, but most nurseries and reception classes will have:

- long-term plans;
- medium-term plans;
- short-term plans; and
- plans for individual children.

Planning moves through a number of stages. It goes from long-term planning, which outlines the experiences that children will have over the course of the year, to medium-term plans, which outline the learning objectives for each block of work, to short-term plans, which show the activities that will be offered to children each week. In addition it is sometimes necessary to draw up individual plans for some children, such as those with special educational needs.

Long-term plans

Long-term plans provide an overview of the range of learning opportunities that will be offered to the children over the course of a year or the whole Foundation Stage. They set out what the children will learn in broad terms.

Long-term aims

Long-term plans often include some general aims for the children's learning. These indicate the practitioners' priorities and are likely to have an influence on what and how children will learn. They often include the children's attitudes to learning and may be related to the dispositions they want to foster. Examples of long-term aims might include:

- Children should be able to use oral language confidently when talking to others.
- Children should be able to listen to others, to learn from them and respect their point of view.
- Children should regard reading as a pleasurable and useful activity.
- Children should be able to read and respond to fiction, non-fiction, poetry and song texts in a variety of media.
- Children should understand that writing has a variety of purposes and uses in everyday life.

■ Children should understand that some writing benefits from being planned and altered.

Themes and topics

In the Foundation Stage it is common for practitioners to show the themes or topics that will be covered by the class during the year on their long-term plans. The topics that are selected provide a context for all the children's learning during a period of time and help to ensure coherence and integration of learning. Topics can be chosen for their relevance to the children in the setting and their particular community, as well as being selected for their potential to widen the children's experiences. Long-term plans also show special events that can add to the theme and provide starting points for learning. These might include festivals, visits or visitors. Topics can last for different lengths of time. Some will last for three or four weeks and some for half a term. Common topics in the Foundation Stage include:

■ All about me;
■ Journeys;
■ Nursery Rhymes;
■ Celebration;
■ Holidays;
■ Growth;
■ A single book;
■ Books by a single author;
■ Markets; and
■ Storytelling.

Each of these topics might be especially suited to one of the areas of learning for example *Growth* would be particularly appropriate to learning in the Physical Development and Personal, Social and Emotional Development areas of learning and *Journeys* would be particularly suited to Knowledge and Understanding of the World. However, all the themes will include plenty of opportunities for learning about the six aspects of learning that comprise communication, language and literacy.

Timing and progression

Long-term plans are usually drawn up by teams of practitioners working together. This might be all the staff who work in the nursery or it could be the combined staff of the nursery and reception class. Practitioners will want to avoid repetition of topics and resources and to make sure that there is progression between nursery and reception classes so it is wise to collaborate when selecting themes and topics. For the same reasons the plans for the Foundation Stage will also be shared with Year 1 teachers.

Long-term plans should include:

- an indication of when each aspect of each area of learning is going to be taught;
- an indication of how regularly and frequently each aspect of each area of learning will be covered;
- an indication of how aspects and areas of learning will be linked and made relevant and interesting for the children;
- special events and activities that provide a meaningful context and enhance learning; and
- the time allocated to each topic.

In order to ensure that during their time in the Foundation Stage children will experience a broad, balanced and progressive curriculum, practitioners usually check that long-term plans:

- include all aspects of learning;
- maintain a balance between and within the six areas of learning; and
- provide sufficient opportunities for children to revisit all aspects of learning regularly and frequently.

Figure 8.1 shows what an extract from a long-term plan for a nursery might look like. More details could be added particularly in the resources section. Figures 8.2 and 8.4, 8.5 and 8.6 which appear later in this chapter as medium-term and short-term plans give more detail about the storytelling topic.

Medium-term plans

Once the set of topics for the year has been selected and practitioners agree that these topics will enable the children to cover all the aspects of each area of learning in a coherent and balanced way, it is possible to draw up medium-term plans. These contain objectives which are linked to the themes and aspects of learning in the long-term plan. The objectives, taken from the stepping stones, the Early Learning Goals (QCA, 2000b) or the *National Literacy Strategy: Framework for Teaching* (DfES, 2001a), will not be achievable by all the children in just one or two sessions; they will need to be revisited during the course of the theme. They should, however, be achievable by most of the children over a period of weeks.

Autumn term				
Topic	Main areas of learning	Main aspects of learning	Special events	Resources
All about me	Personal, social, and emotional development	Self-confidence and self-esteem Making relationships Self-care Sense of community	Visit from a parent with a young baby	Role play – baby clinic, hospital, health centre Books – *What do I Look Like?* by Nick Sharratt *The Baby's Catalogue* by Allan Ahlberg *Alfie's Alphabet* by Shirley Hughes Other resources – Photographs, names
	Knowledge and understanding of the world	Sense of time Cultures and beliefs		
	Physical development	Health and bodily awareness		
Markets	Mathematical development	Numbers as labels and for counting Calculating	Visit to market	Role play – market stalls outside Other resources – environmental print
Story-telling	Communication, language and literacy	Language for communication Language for thinking Reading Writing		See Figures 8.2, 8.4, 8.5 and 8.6 for more details
	Creative development	Imagination		
Celebration	Creative development	Exploring media and materials Music	End-of-term party End-of-term event for parents and friends	Books – *Spot's First Christmas* by Eric Hill Other resources – greetings cards, posters, invitations, lists, menus
	Physical development	Movement Using tools and materials		

Figure 8.1 *An extract from the long-term plans for a nursery class*

A medium-term plan will cover the duration of one of the topics that has been selected so it could cover a period of between three and six weeks. Medium-term plans contain a little more detail about the way in which the objectives will be taught, and they begin to situate the learning in contexts that are meaningful, relevant and appropriate to the children. An important aspect of medium-term planning is to think of the outcomes for the topic. These should be outcomes that the children can recognize so that they can see that their work has been significant and respected. The outcomes should give children tangible evidence of their learning and help them to feel proud of what they have achieved.

There are six aspects of communication, language and literacy that need to be covered in the medium-term plan. These are:

- language for communication;
- language for thinking;
- linking sounds and letters;
- reading;
- writing; and
- handwriting.

Each of these elements will need to be planned for. The DfES (PNS, 2004) has produced some sample medium-term plans for the Foundation Stage which include all six elements and which cluster the objectives taken from stepping stones and Early Learning Goals in a helpful and coherent manner. The plans ensure that all aspects of communication, language and literacy and all the stepping stones and Early Learning Goals are covered and revisited in a balanced way during the course of a year. They suggest some possible activities and outcomes for the block of work, but practitioners are free to choose their own starting points and plan their own curriculum when they translate the medium-term plans into their own short-term plans. The objectives are taken from the different levels of learning within each aspect confirming that children will be at different stages of development and so different learning outcomes will be expected. One of the virtues of the sample Primary National Strategy (PNS) plans is that they remind us that good planning and good teaching begin with knowing what we want children to learn and, therefore, the plans should start with identifying learning objectives. Once these are known, practitioners can begin to think creatively about activities and experiences that will enable children to learn what is required. Even if one does not use the PNS plans they are a useful illustration of how to go about producing medium-term plans for communication, language and literacy. Figures 8.2 and 8.3 show the PNS sample plans, one for a nursery class and

Earlier Foundation Stage

Storytelling [reading and talk] e.g. Tell me a story	Possible resources/activities Retell and create using: • story boxes • props and puppets • sequencing cards and pictures	Possible links with other areas of learning Creative development • e.g. use their imagination in role play and stories empathising with characters
	• role-play/home corner (dressing-up) • masks and story maps • circle stories • storyteller's chair	

Sounds and handwriting

Language for communication, thinking and reading

Sounds

Stepping Stones
Linking sounds and letters p.60–61
Yellow:
• Enjoy rhyming and rhythmic activities
• Distinguish one sound from another
Blue:
• Show awareness of rhyme and alliteration
• Recognise rhyme in spoken words
Green:
• Continue a rhyming string
• Hear and say the initial sound in words and know which letters represent some of the sounds

Progression in phonics
Step 1 General sound discrimination, Speech sound discrimination, Rhythm and rhyme, Alliteration
Step 2 Learning objectives:
Rhyming string, Hear and say initial phonemes

Stepping Stones
Language for communication p.50–51
Yellow:
• Listen to favourite nursery rhymes, stories and songs. Join in with repeated refrains, anticipating key events and important phrases
• Respond to simple instructions
• Listen to others in one-to-one/small groups when conversation interests them
Blue:
• Listen to stories with increasing attention and recall
• Describe main story settings, events and principal characters
• Question why things happen, and give explanations
Green:
• Initiate a conversation, negotiate positions, pay attention to and take account of others' views

Language for communication p.52–53
Yellow:
• Use familiar words, often in isolation, to identify what they do and do not want
• Use vocabulary focused on objects and people who are of particular importance to them
Blue:
• Build up vocabulary that reflects the breadth of their experiences
• Begin to experiment with language describing possession
Green:
• Extend vocabulary, especially by grouping and naming
• Use vocabulary and forms of speech that are increasingly influenced by experience of books

Handwriting
Stepping Stones p. 66–67
Yellow:
• Engage in activities requiring hand-eye coordination
• Use one-handed tools and equipment
Blue:
• Draw lines and circles using gross motor movement
• Manipulate objects with increasing control
Green:
• Begin to use anticlockwise movement and retrace vertical lines
• Begin to form recognisable letters

Developing early writing p.156–164

Language for thinking p.56–59
Blue:
• Use talk, actions and objects to recall and relive past experiences
Green:
• Begin to use talk to pretend imaginary situations

Reading p.62–63
Yellow:
• Listen to and join in with stories and poems, one-to-one and also in small groups
• Begin to be aware of the way stories are structured
Blue:
• Suggest how the story might end

Figure 8.2 *A sample medium-term plan for communication, language and literacy for the early Foundation Stage (PNS, 2004: 3)*

Narrative: predictable structures and patterned language e.g. Tell me a story	Possible texts and materials • Stories with predictable structures and patterned language	Possible outcome(s) • Retelling stories using a variety of props and artefacts • Puppet plays • Story boards • Mini-books

Phonics and handwriting

Linking sounds and letters

Stepping Stones

Linking sounds and letters p.60-61
- Enjoy rhyming and rhythmic activities (yellow)
- Distinguish one sound from another (yellow)
- Show awareness of rhyme and alliteration (blue)
- Recognise rhyme in spoken words (blue)
- Continue a rhyming string (green)
- Hear and say the initial sound in words and know which letters represent some of the sounds (green)

Progression in phonics
Step 1 General sound discrimination, Speech sound discrimination, Rhythm and rhyme, Alliteration
Step 2 Learning objectives
to be able to continue a rhyming string
to hear and say phonemes /s/, /m/, /k/, /l/, /g/, /h/ in initial position
to know phoneme-grapheme correspondences: s, m, c, l, g, h
Step 3 (as appropriate)

Handwriting

Stepping Stones p.66-67
- Engage in activities requiring hand-eye coordination (yellow)
- Use one-handed tools and equipment (yellow)
- Draw lines and circles using gross motor movement (blue)
- Manipulate objects with increasing control (blue)
- Begin to use anticlockwise movement and retrace vertical lines (green)
- Begin to form recognisable letters (green)

NLS YR objectives
W12 to use a comfortable and efficient pencil grip;
W13 to produce a controlled line which supports letter formation;
W14 to write letters using the correct sequence of movements. (*Developing early writing* p.156-164)

Word level objectives

Word recognition, graphic knowledge and spelling

Stepping Stones

Reading p.62-63
- Understand the concept of a word (blue)
- Begin to recognise some familiar words (green)

NLS YR objectives
W6 to read on sight the 45 high frequency words to be taught by the end of YR from Appendix List 1;
W7 to read on sight the words from texts of appropriate difficulty;
W9 to recognise the critical features of words, e.g: shape, length, and common spelling patterns.

Vocabulary extension

Stepping Stones

Language for communication p.52-53
- Use familiar words, often in isolation, to identify what they do and do not want (yellow)
- Use vocabulary focused on objects and people who are of particular importance to them (yellow)
- Extend vocabulary, especially by grouping and naming (green)

NLS YR objectives
W10 new words from their reading and shared experiences.

Figure 8.3 *A sample medium-term plan for communication, language and literacy for the later Foundation Stage (PNS, 2004: 0–11)*

Narrative: predictable structures and patterned language (continued)

Text and sentence level objectives

Stepping Stones

Language for communication p.48-49

- Use words and/or gestures, including body language such as eye contact and facial expression, to communicate (yellow)
- Use intonation, rhythm and phrasing to make their meaning clear to others (blue)
- Use simple grammatical structures (green)
- Ask simple questions, often in the form of 'where' or 'what' (green)

Language for communication p.50-51

- Listen to favourite nursery rhymes, stories and songs. Join in with repeated refrains, anticipating key events and important phrases (yellow)
- Listen to others in one-to-one/small groups when conversation interests them (yellow)
- Listen to stories with increasing attention and recall (blue)
- Describe main story settings, events and principal characters (blue)
- Initiate a conversation, negotiate positions, pay attention to and take account of others' views (green)

Language for communication p.54-55

- Begin to use more complex sentences (blue)
- Use a widening range of words to express or elaborate ideas (blue)
- Link statements and stick to a main theme or intention (green)
- Consistently develop a simple story, explanation or line of questioning (green)

Language for thinking p. 56-59

- Begin to use talk instead of action to rehearse, reorder and reflect on past experience, linking significant events from own experience and from stories, paying attention to sequence and how events lead into one another (yellow)
- Begin to use talk to pretend imaginary situations (yellow)

Reading p.62-63

- Begin to use more complex sentences (blue)
- Use a widening range of words to express or elaborate ideas (blue)
- Link statements and stick to a main theme or intention (green)
- Consistently develop a simple story, explanation or line of questioning (green)

Writing p.64-65

- Ascribe meanings to marks (blue)
- Begin to break the flow of speech into words (green)
- Use writing as a means of recording and communicating (green)

NLS YR text level objectives

T1 through shared reading:

a) to recognise printed and handwritten words in a variety of settings, e.g. stories, notes, registers, labels, signs, notices, letters, forms, lists, directions, advertisements, newspapers;

b) that words can be written down to be read again for a wide range of purposes;

c) to track the text in the right order, page by page, left to right, top to bottom; pointing while reading/telling a story, and making one-to-one correspondences between written and spoken words;

T6 to re-read frequently a variety of familiar texts, e.g. big books, story books, taped stories with texts, poems, information books, wall stories, captions, own and other children's writing;

T7 to use knowledge of familiar texts to re-enact or re-tell to others, recounting the main points in correct sequence;

T10 to re-read and recite stories and rhymes with predictable and repeated patterns and experiment with similar rhyming patterns;

T11 through shared writing:

a) to understand that writing can be used for a range of purposes, e.g. to send messages, record, inform, tell stories;

b) to understand that writing remains constant, i.e. will always 'say' the same thing;

c) to understand how writing is formed directionally, a word at a time;

T12 through guided and independent writing:

a) to experiment with writing in a variety of play, exploratory and role-play situations.

NLS YR sentence level objectives

S1 to expect written text to make sense and to check for sense if it does not;

S2 to understand that writing can be used for a range of purposes, e.g. to send messages, record, inform, tell stories.

one for a reception class. Figure 8.2 is based on the topic of story-telling and expands on the example of story-telling that was given in the sample long-term plan in Figure 8.1.

Short-term planning

Short-term plans usually show the activities and objectives that will be worked on over the course of a week. They specify where adults will work, independent activities and activities that are suited to assessing pupils' progress. They will indicate links with other curriculum areas and identify when special events will take place. To produce a short-term plan practitioners need to begin with the objectives from the medium-term plan and then think of activities and experiences that will enable these objectives to be realized during each week for the duration of the topic. They contain a balance between learning objectives and valuable activities. Thinking of relevant and stimulating activities allows practitioners to find creative and imaginative ways to interpret the curriculum.

Nursery plans

Practitioners do not have to work with the Primary National Strategy medium-term plans but I have taken the 'Story-telling' medium-term plan for the earlier Foundation Stage (Figure 8.2) and broken this down into three weekly or short-term plans for communication, language and literacy to show what short-term plans might look like. These are included as Figures 8.4, 8.5 and 8.6. I have based all the learning related to the 'Story-telling' topic on one book, *Rosie's Walk* by Pat Hutchins (1970). When planning, it is important to think about the order and the pace of the activities. Some activities will need to precede others. For example on the *Rosie's Walk* plan (Figure 8.4) the children need to make the equipment for the outdoor play area before they can act out and retell the story outside. It is also important to allow children time to explore new activities and to repeat some activities in order to give children the opportunity to develop and consolidate their learning. However, children can find too much repetition dull, so practitioners need to make judgements about what is appropriate to the children's needs and interests.

On the plans I have indicated the learning intentions for each activity, a brief description of each activity indicating whether it is adult led, where it will take place and the resources and equipment that will be needed. There are some gaps on the plans and these would be filled with activities linked to the other five areas of learning. If these plans were being used they would also need to show:

- which adults are responsible for the activities;
- which activities provide opportunities for observation and assessment of children; and
- questions and vocabulary that might be used by adults during the activities.

Reception plans

Short-term plans for reception classes may have a different format to that used in nurseries. They are likely to make more use of the literacy hour teaching strategies and, towards the end of the reception year, much of the teaching for communication, language and literacy will occur in a daily hour. In the sample 2 week plan which follows (Figure 8.7) there are a number of independent and play activities but there is regular use of shared reading and writing, group reading and writing, and whole-class phonic work. The objectives listed on the plan are taken from the *Draft Framework for Teaching Literacy* (PNS, 2006). The starting point for the sample reception plan is the short film, *The Lucky Dip* (bfi education, 2003b). This tells the story of a young girl's visit to the seaside and would fit in with the topic of 'Holidays'. In addition to the activities shown on the plan there should be regular opportunities for children and adults to read together individually and daily story times when books, poems and songs are shared with the class.

Activity
Assume that you are the teacher responsible for the reception class who are following *The Lucky Dip* plan. During literacy sessions a teaching assistant works with your class. Which activities would benefit from being led by an adult? Which activities would provide information about children's learning and so could be identified as good assessment opportunities? Finally, how might you keep track of the activities the children had completed and make sure that they all produced a completed and extended storyboard as well as contributing to the wall story display?

Planning for role play

In order to get the best out of a role-play area, many Foundation Stage practitioners draw up a separate plan for the role-play area. This ensures that it covers specific learning objectives, that resources can be prepared in good

Theme 'Storytelling' based on *Rosie's Walk* by Pat Hutchins	Week 1			
	Monday	Tuesday	Wednesday	Thursday	Friday
Sand tray	Resource the sand tray with farm animals and props to encourage the children to play with the story. Learning objectives *Language for Thinking Green: Begin to use talk to pretend imaginary situations* *Language for Thinking Grey: Use language to imagine and re-create roles and experiences*			Resource the sand tray with farm animals and props to encourage the children to play with the story. Learning objectives *Language for Thinking Green: Begin to use talk to pretend imaginary situations* *Language for Thinking Grey: Use language to imagine and re-create roles and experiences*	
Water tray					
Writing area			Make repeating patterns using single letters eg a row of hhhhh Some of these can be used to decorate the class book in week 3. Learning objectives *Handwriting Green: Begin to form recognizable letters* *Handwriting Grey: Use a pencil and hold it effectively to form recognizable letters, most of which are correctly formed*		
Reading area	Make sure copies of *Rosie's Walk* and other books that are read during the theme are available for the children to read Learning objectives *Reading Green: Enjoy an increasing range of books* *Reading Grey: Explore and experiment with sounds, words and texts*				
Listening area	Make a story tape of the text in *Rosie's Walk*. Put this in the listening area along with 2 copies of the book to give children the opportunity to return to and 'read' the book themselves.			Make a story tape of the text in *Rosie's Walk*. Put this in the listening area along with 2 copies of the book to give children the opportunity to return to and 'read' the book themselves.	

Figure 8.4 *Short-term plan for 'Storytelling' based on* Rosie's Walk, *week 1*

Theme 'Storytelling' based on *Rosie's Walk* by Pat Hutchins   Week 1 – continued

	Monday	Tuesday	Wednesday	Thursday	Friday
	Learning objectives *Reading Yellow:* *Listen to and join in with stories and poems; one-to-one and also in small groups* *Reading Green: Begin to recognize some familiar words* *Reading Grey: Read a range of familiar and common words and simple sentences independently*			Learning objectives *Reading Yellow:* *Listen to and join in with stories and poems; one-to-one and also in small groups* *Reading Green: Begin to recognize some familiar words* *Reading Grey: Read a range of familiar and common words and simple sentences independently*	
Creative area	Adult and children work together to draw and colour a story map. Opportunity to reflect on, discuss and retell the story. The children can use the map for small-world play with farmyard animals Hencoop, yard, pond, haycock, mill, fence, beehives, (hencoop) Learning objectives *Reading Yellow:* *Begin to be aware of the way stories are structured* *Reading Grey: Retell narratives in the correct sequence, drawing on language pattern of stories* Links with Creative Development	Large 3D story props (made our of boxes for use outside) Children decorate the boxes to make each of the places Rosie passes. Children work in 2s/3s to do this. Link with CD. When finished the props can be used to re-enact the story. Learning objective *Reading Grey: Retell narratives in the correct sequence, drawing on language pattern of stories* Links with Creative Development		Adult and children work together to draw and colour a story map. Opportunity to reflect on, discuss and retell the story. The children can use the map for small-world play with farmyard animals Hencoop, yard, pond, haycock, mill, fence, beehives, (hencoop) Learning objectives *Reading Yellow:* *Begin to be aware of the way stories are structured* *Reading Grey: Retell narratives in the correct sequence, drawing on language pattern of stories* Links with Creative Development	
Sensory area	Use wet cornflour to make repeating patterns using single letters eg a row of hhhh, a row of eeee, a row of nnnn. Learning objectives *Handwriting Yellow: Engage in activities requiring hand-eye coordination* *Handwriting Green: Begin to form recognizable letters*		Use wet cornflour to make repeating patterns using single letters eg a row of hhhh, a row of eeee, a row of nnnn. Learning objectives *Handwriting Yellow: Engage in activities requiring hand-eye coordination* *Handwriting Green: Begin to form recognizable letters*		
Imaginative play area					
Small-world play					

Theme 'Storytelling' based on *Rosie's Walk* by Pat Hutchins   Week 1 — continued

	Monday	Tuesday	Wednesday	Thursday	Friday
Outdoor area					
ICT					
Small group time	Play a game with the children. You will need a toy hen. Tell the children to close their eyes and then ask 'Is Rosie under the book?', 'behind the chair?' etc. This will encourage their use of positional language, something that is emphasized in the book. Invite individual children to hide Rosie and the rest of the class to guess where she is. They must use positional language in their guesses. Learning objectives *Language for communication Green: Extend vocabulary, especially by grouping and naming* *Language for communication Green: Use vocabulary and forms of speech that are increasingly influenced by experience of books* Links with Mathematical Development		Discuss words that rhyme with 'hen' – Ben, den, fen, men, pen, ten, Write these as a list and discuss sounds and letters (onset and rime). Make some silly sentences or phrases, e.g., 'The hen picked up the pen' Learning objectives *Linking sounds and letters Green: Continue a rhyming string* *Linking sounds and letters Green: Hear and say the initial sound in words and know which letters represent some of the sounds*		
Large group time		Read other stories by Pat Hutchins to the children. Do this during the 3 week block. Read similar stories, e.g. *Suddenly* by Colin McNaughton, *Handa's Surprise* by Eileen Browne Learning objectives *Reading Blue: Listen to stories with increasing attention and recall* *Reading Green: Enjoy an increasing range of books*		In shared writing creating some thought bubbles to show what Rosie and/or the fox are thinking at different points in the story. These could be used as part of a display. Learning objectives *Writing Green: Begin to break the flow of speech into words* *Writing Green: Use writing as a means of recording and communicating* *Writing Grey: Attempt writing for different purposes, using features of different forms such as lists; stories and instructions*	Read other stories by Pat Hutchins to the children. Do this during the 3 week block. Read similar stories eg *Suddenly* by Colin McNaughton, *Handa's Surprise* by Eileen Browne Learning objective *Reading Blue: Listen to stories with increasing attention and recall* *Reading Green: Enjoy an increasing range of books*

Theme 'Storytelling' based on *Rosie's Walk* by Pat Hutchins   Week 2

	Monday	Tuesday	Wednesday	Thursday	Friday
Sand tray	Resource the sand tray with farm animals and props to encourage the children to play with the story. Learning objectives *Language for Thinking Green: Begin to use talk to pretend imaginary situations* *Language for Thinking Grey: Use language to imagine and re-create roles and experiences*			Resource the sand tray with farm animals and props to encourage the children to play with the story. Learning objectives *Language for Thinking Green: Begin to use talk to pretend imaginary situations* *Language for Thinking Grey: Use language to imagine and re-create roles and experiences*	
Water tray					
Writing area			Make repeating patterns using single letters, a row of eeeee Some of these can be used to decorate the class book in week 3. Learning objectives *Handwriting Green: Begin to form recognizable letters* *Handwriting Grey: Use a pencil and hold it effectively to form recognizable letters, most of which are correctly formed*		Work with groups of children to make a simple rhyming pairs game using pictures cut out from comics, magazines and catalogues. Children should play the game. Learning objectives *Linking sounds and letters Green: Continue a rhyming string* *Linking sounds and letters Green: Hear and say the initial sound in words and know which letters represent some of the sounds*
Reading area	Make sure copies of *Rosie's Walk* and other books that are read during the theme are available for the children to read. Learning objectives *Reading Green: Enjoy an increasing range of books* *Reading Grey: Explore and experiment with sounds, words and texts*				
Listening area	Make a story tape of the text in *Rosie's Walk*. Put this in the listening area along with 2 copies of the book to give children the opportunity to return to and 'read' the book themselves. Learning objectives *Reading Yellow:* *Listen to and join in with stories and poems, one-to-one and also in small groups* *Reading Green: Begin to recognize some familiar words*			Make a story tape of the text in *Rosie's Walk*. Put this in the listening area along with 2 copies of the book to give children the opportunity to return to and 'read' the book themselves. Learning objectives *Reading Yellow:* *Listen to and join in with stories and poems, one-to-one and also in small groups* *Reading Green: Begin to recognize some familiar words*	

Figure 8.5 *Short-term plan for 'Storytelling' based on Rosie's Walk, week 2*

Theme 'Storytelling' based on *Rosie's Walk* by Pat Hutchins   Week 2 – continued

	Monday	Tuesday	Wednesday	Thursday	Friday
	Reading Grey: Read a range of familiar and common words and simple sentences independently			*Reading Grey: Read a range of familiar and common words and simple sentences independently*	
Creative area	Adult and children work together to draw and colour a story map. Opportunity to reflect on, discuss and retell the story. The children can use the map for small-world play with farmyard animals Hencoop, yard, pond, haycock, mill, fence, beehives, (hencoop) Learning objectives *Reading Yellow:* *Begin to be aware of the way stories are structured* *Reading Grey: Retell narratives in the correct sequence, drawing on language pattern of stories*		Children produce illustrations for the class book Learning objectives *Reading Yellow: Show interest in illustration and print in books and print in the environment* *Handwriting Blue: Manipulate objects with increasing control* Links with Creative Development	Adult and children work together to make a track game of *Rosie's Walk*. Use the story map from week 1 to help. Label the items that you include – hencoop, yard, pond, etc to provide children with models of written words. Children play this game in 2s or 3s with an adult. Learning objectives *Reading Green: Begin to recognize some familiar words* *Reading Grey: Read a range of familiar and common words and simple sentences independently*	
Sensory area	Use wet cornflour to make repeating patterns using single letters, e.g. a row of hhhhh, a row of eeeee, a row of nnnnn Learning objectives *Handwriting Yellow: Engage in activities requiring hand–eye coordination* *Handwriting Green: Begin to form recognizable letters*			Use wet cornflour to make repeating patterns using single letters, e.g. a row of hhhhh, a row of eeeee, a row of nnnnn. Learning objectives *Handwriting Yellow: Engage in activities requiring handeye coordination* *Handwriting Green: Begin to form recognizable letters*	
Imaginative play area					
Small-world play		Use story boxes for containing items from *Rosie's Walk* for children to re-create the story and create their own stories Learning objectives *Reading Yellow: Begin to be aware of the way stories are structured* *Reading Grey: Retell narratives in the correct sequence, drawing on language patterns of stories*			
Outdoor area		Large 3D story props made by children used to re-enact the story *Rosie's Walk* Learning objective		Large 3D story props made by children used to re-enact the story *Rosie's Walk* Learning objective	

Theme 'Storytelling' based on *Rosie's Walk* by Pat Hutchins   Week 2 – continued

	Monday	Tuesday	Wednesday	Thursday	Friday
		Reading Grey: Retell narratives in the correct sequence, drawing on language pattern of stories Links with Creative Development		*Reading Grey: Retell narratives in the correct sequence, drawing on language pattern of stories* Links with Creative Development	
ICT					
Small group time	Play a game with the children. You will need a toy hen. Tell the children to close their eyes and then ask 'Is Rosie under the book?', 'behind the chair?' etc. This will encourage their use of positional language, something that is emphasized in the book. Invite individual children to hide Rosie and the rest of the class to guess where she is. They must use positional language in their guesses. Link with MD. Learning objectives *Language for communication Green: Extend vocabulary, especially by grouping and naming* *Language for communication Green: Use vocabulary and forms of speech that are increasingly influenced by experience of books*		Discuss words that rhyme with 'hen' – Ben, den, fen, men, pen, ten. Write these as a list and discuss sounds and letters (onset and time) Learning objectives *Linking sounds and letters Green: Continue a rhyming string* *Linking sounds and letters Green: Hear and say the initial sound in words and know which letters represent some of the sounds*		Make a set of sequencing cards that show Rosie next to each of the farmyard features that she passes. The children can use these to retell the story. Learning objective *Reading Grey: Retell narratives in the correct sequence, drawing on language patterns of stories*
Large group time	Make a class book that retells Rosie's story. The teacher does the writing the children produce the illustrations. Learning objective *Writing Grey: Attempt writing for different purposes, using features of different forms such as lists, stories and instructions*	Read other stories by Pat Hutchins to the children. Do this during the 3 week block. Read similar stories, e.g. *Suddenly* by Colin McNaughton, *Handa's Surprise* by Eileen Browne Learning objectives *Reading Blue: Listen to stories with increasing attention and recall* *Reading Green: Enjoy an increasing range of books*			Read other stories by Pat Hutchins to the children. Do this during the 3 week block. Read similar stories, e.g. *Suddenly* by Colin McNaughton, *Handa's Surprise* by Eileen Browne Learning objectives *Reading Blue: Listen to stories with increasing attention and recall* *Reading Green: Enjoy an increasing range of books*

Theme 'Storytelling' based on *Rosie's Walk* by Pat Hutchins	Week 3				
	Monday	Tuesday	Wednesday	Thursday	Friday
Sand tray	Resource the sand tray with farm animals and props to encourage the children to play with the story. Learning objectives *Language for Thinking Green: Begin to use talk to pretend imaginary situations* *Language for Thinking Grey: Use language to imagine and recreate roles and experiences*			Resource the sand tray with farm animals and props to encourage the children to play with the story. Learning objectives *Language for Thinking Green: Begin to use talk to pretend imaginary situations* *Language for Thinking Grey: Use language to imagine and recreate roles and experiences*	
Water tray					
Writing area		Resource this so that children can make their own books similar to the class book – *Cath's Walk*. They could make their own *Tom's Walk*, *Charlotte's Walk*, etc. Learning objective *Writing Grey: Attempt writing for different purposes, using features of different forms such as lists, stories and instructions*	Make repeating patterns using single letters, a row of nnnn. Some of these can be used to decorate the class book in week 3. Learning objectives *Handwriting Green: Begin to form recognizable letters* *Handwriting Grey: Use a pencil and hold it effectively to form recognizable letters, most of which are correctly formed*	Resource this so that children can make their own books similar to the class book – *Cath's Walk*. They could make their own *Tom's Walk*, *Charlotte's Walk*, etc. Learning objective *Writing Grey: Attempt writing for different purposes, using features of different forms such as lists, stories and instructions*	
Reading area	Make sure copies of *Rosie's Walk* and other books that are read during the theme are available for the children to read. Learning objectives *Reading Green: Enjoy an increasing range of books* *Reading Grey: Explore and experiment with sounds, words and texts*				
Listening area	Make a story tape of the text in *Rosie's Walk*. Put this in the listening area along with 2 copies of the book to give children the opportunity to return to and 'read' the book themselves. Learning objectives			Make a story tape of the text in *Rosie's Walk*. Put this in the listening area along with 2 copies of the book to give children the opportunity to return to and 'read' the book themselves. Learning objectives	

Figure 8.6 *Short-term plan for 'Storytelling' based on Rosie's Walk, week 3*

Theme 'Storytelling' based on *Rosie's Walk* by Pat Hutchins   Week 3 – continued

	Monday	Tuesday	Wednesday	Thursday	Friday
	Reading Yellow: Listen to and join in with stories and poems, one-to-one and also in small groups *Reading Green: Begin to recognize some familiar words* *Reading Grey: Read a range of familiar and common words and simple sentences independently*			*Reading Yellow:* Listen to and join in with stories and poems, one-to-one and also in small groups *Reading Green: Begin to recognize some familiar words* *Reading Grey: Read a range of familiar and common words and simple sentences independently*	Friday
Creative area			Children produce illustrations for the class book Learning objectives *Reading Yellow: Show interest in illustration and print in books and print in the environment* *Handwriting Blue: Manipulate objects with increasing control* Links with Creative Development		
Sensory area	Use wet cornflour to make repeating patterns using single letters eg a row of hhhhh, a row of eeee, a row of nnnn Learning objectives *Handwriting Yellow: Engage in activities requiring hand-eye coordination* *Handwriting Green: Begin to form recognizable letters*			Use wet cornflour to make repeating patterns using single letters eg a row of hhhhh, a row of eeee, a row of nnnn. Learning objectives *Handwriting Yellow: Engage in activities requiring hand-eye coordination* *Handwriting Green: Begin to form recognizable letters*	
Imaginative play area	The children make face masks either the fox or Rosie. These can be used for the children to retell the story from the perspective of Rosie or the fox during a large class session (modelling). Later the children can use them in conjunction with the large outdoor story props. Learning objective *Language for thinking Grey: Use language to imagine and re-create roles and experiences*		The children make face masks either the fox or Rosie. These can be used for the children to retell the story from the perspective of Rosie or the fox during a large class session (modelling). Later the children can use them in conjunction with the large outdoor story props. Learning objective *Language for thinking Grey: Use language to imagine and re-create roles and experiences*		

Theme 'Storytelling' based on *Rosie's Walk* by Pat Hutchins   Week 3 – continued

	Monday	Tuesday	Wednesday	Thursday	Friday
Small-world play	Links with Creative Development	Use story boxes for combining items from *Rosie's Walk* for children to re-create the story and create their own stories. Learning objectives *Reading Yellow: Begin to be aware of the way stories are structured* *Reading Grey: Retell narratives in the correct sequence, drawing on language patterns of stories*	Links with Creative Development		
Outdoor area		Large 3D story props made by children used to re-enact the story *Rosie's Walk.* Incorporate masks. Learning objective *Reading Grey: Retell narratives in the correct sequence, drawing on language pattern of stories* Links with Creative Development		Large 3D story props made by children used to re-enact the story *Rosie's Walk.* Incorporate masks. Learning objective *Reading Grey: Retell narratives in the correct sequence, drawing on language pattern of stories* Links with Creative Development	
ICT					
Small group time	Play a game with the children. You will need a toy hen. Tell the children to close their eyes and then ask 'Is Rosie under the book?', 'behind the chair?' etc. This will encourage their use of positional language, something that is emphasized in the book. Invite individual children to hide Rosie and the rest of the class to guess where she is. They must use positional language in their guesses. Link with M9. Learning objectives *Language for communication Green: Extend vocabulary, especially by grouping and naming* *Language for communication Green: Use*		Discuss words that rhyme with 'fox' – box, locks, ox, rocks, socks. Write these as a list and discuss sounds and letters (onset and rime) Discuss the different ways that 'ox' can be written. Make some silly sentences or phrases, e.g. 'The ox hid in a box' Learning objectives *Linking sounds and letters Green: Continue a rhyming string* *Linking sounds and letters Green: Hear and say the initial sound in words and know which letters represent some of the sounds* *Linking sounds and letters Grey: Link sounds to letters, naming and sounding letters of the alphabet*		Make a set of sequencing cards that show Rosie next to each of the farmyard features that she passes. The children can use these to re-tell the story. Learning objective *Reading Grey: Re-tell narratives in the correct sequence, drawing on language patterns of stories*

Theme 'Storytelling' based on *Rosie's Walk* by Pat Hutchins   Week 3 – continued

	Monday	Tuesday	Wednesday	Thursday	Friday
	vocabulary and forms of speech that are increasingly influenced by experience of books				
Large group time	Make a class book of an imaginary walk around the classroom — inside and outdoors. Introduce this as an oral story during whole class/large group time. The children can suggest significant items in the classroom. Onto the teacher went for a walk, Across the carpet Around the blocks, Over the climbing frame, etc. As a group activity the children can draw a classroom item. This should be labelled in front of them so that they see models of writing. Collect the illustrations and write the text and mount the illustrations. Read the book with the children. Link to CD. Learning objective *Reading Grey: Explore and experiment with sounds, words and texts* Link to Creative Development, Physical Development and Mathematical Development	Read other stories by Pat Hutchins to the children. Do this during the 3 week block. Read similar stories, e.g. *Suddenly* by Colin McNaughton, *Handa's Surprise* by Eileen Browne Learning objectives *Reading Blue: Listen to stories with increasing attention and recall* *Reading Green: Enjoy an increasing range of books*	Make a class book of an imaginary walk around the classroom — inside and outdoors. Introduce this as an oral story during whole class/large group time. The children can suggest significant items in the classroom. Onto the teacher went for a walk, Across the carpet Around the blocks, Over the climbing frame, etc. As a group activity the children can draw a classroom item. This should be labelled in front of them so that they see models of writing. Collect the illustrations and write the text and mount the illustrations. Read the book with the children. Link to CD. Learning objective *Reading Grey: Explore and experiment with sounds, words and texts* Link to Creative Development, Physical Development and Mathematical Development		Read the class book. Encourage the children to join in. Learning objectives *Reading Green: Enjoy an increasing range of books* *Begin to recognize some familiar words* *Reading Grey: Retell narratives in the correct sequence, drawing on the language patterns of stories*

Plan for Communication, language and literacy   Reception   Summer term

Narrative: Structure
Text: *The Lucky Dip* by Emily Skinner 2001 from Starting Stories Video, British Film Institute
Wall story display
Timescale: 2 weeks

Other books to read: *Come away from the water, Shirley!* (Burningham), *Spot goes on Holiday* (Hill), *The Sandcastle, The Big Sea, Seaside Poems* (Bennett), *The Little Boat* (Henderson), *Lucy and Tom at the Seaside* (Hughes), *Oh I do like to be beside the seaside* (written and composed by John A. Glover-Kind, 1907)

Week 1

	Whole-class work	Group activities	Plenary
Monday	Discuss seaside. What is it like? What do we see there? What do we do there? Use talk partners. Look at pictures and postcards. Can we add anything to our list? Objectives Use language to imagine and re-create roles and experiences Use talk to organize, sequence and clarify thinking, ideas, feelings and events Make a bank of words children will need when writing during the work on *The Lucky Dip.* Objective Read a range of familiar and common words independently	Draw and label a seaside setting Objective Attempt writing for various purposes Write their own names and simple text Sand tray and outdoor sand resourced with buckets, spades, shells, pebbles Water tray resourced with boats, shells, pebbles, play people Objective Use language to imagine and re-create roles and experiences Shallow trays filled with sand for children to practise letter formation Objective Use a pencil and hold it effectively to form recognizable letters, most of which are correctly formed Writing area resourced with postcards and writing implements Objective Attempt writing for various purposes Guided reading Objectives Explore and experiment with sounds, words and texts Show on understanding of the elements of stories, such as main character, sequence of events, and openings	Look at the still of the setting from *The Lucky Dip* and compare it with some of the labelled drawings the children have produced. What is similar? What is different? Objectives Extend their vocabulary, exploring the meanings and sounds of new words Introduce Lucky Dip Game: the aim is to retrieve 3-letter CVC words and read them, blending sounds if necessary. It also introduces children to the idea of a lucky dip which some may not be familiar with. Objectives Blend letters to read CVC words and recognize common digraphs Use their phonic knowledge to read simple regular words Read a range of familiar and common words independently
Tuesday	Watch film up until the little girl falls through the pier. Ask what happens next? Use talk partners. Objectives Show on understanding of the elements of stories, such as main character, sequence of events, and openings Use talk to organize, sequence and clarify thinking, ideas, feelings and events	Sand, water, handwriting trays and writing area resourced as on Monday. Objectives as before Draw and write one sentence to describe what might happen next. Remind children to use word bank. Objectives Attempt writing for various purposes Use their phonic knowledge to write simple regular words and make phonetically plausible attempts at more complex words Guided reading Objectives	Watch the end of the film. Did we expect this? Why and why not? Objectives Show an understanding of the elements of stories, such as main character, sequence of events, and openings Use talk to organize, sequence and clarify thinking, ideas, feelings and events

Figure 8.7 *Short-term plan for 'Holidays' based on* The Lucky Dip

	Whole-class work	Group activities	Plenary
Wednesday	Introduce pictures of the main characters, little girl, pin man, rabbit. How can we describe them? Use talk partners. Explore good, bad, ambivalence. Consider external factors – physical appearance, movement, expression, clothes and internal factors – what they know, how they feel, what they think, how they behave towards others Consider the visual and aural factors that are used in film – close up shots and music Objectives Show an understanding of the elements of stories, such as main character, sequence of events, and openings Interact with others, negotiating plans and activities and taking turns in conversation Use talk to organize, sequence and clarify thinking, ideas, feelings and events Demonstrate through shared writing how to draw and label a character Objective Show an understanding of the elements of stories, such as main character, sequence of events, and openings	Objective Explore and experiment with sounds, words and texts Show an understanding of the elements of stories, such as main character, sequence of events, and openings Sand, water, handwriting trays and writing area resourced as on Monday. Objectives as before In pairs draw and paint large pictures of the characters from the story. These will be used as part of the display. Objectives Sustain attentive listening, responding to what they have heard by relevant comments, questions or actions Interact with others, negotiating plans and activities and taking turns in conversation Draw and label one of the characters from the film Objectives Attempt writing for various purposes Write their own names and simple text Use their phonic knowledge to write simple regular words and make phonetically plausible attempts at more complex words Guided reading Objectives Explore and experiment with sounds, words and texts Show an understanding of the elements of stories, such as main character, sequence of events, and openings	Look at and evaluate some of the character descriptions produced by some children Play the Lucky Dip Game Objectives Blend letters to read CVC words and recognize common digraphs Use their phonic knowledge to read simple regular words Read a range of familiar and common words independently
Thursday	Write pin on whiteboard. Ask children to say the sounds and blend the letters to read the word. Change the p to th, say and remember, change th to ch, say and remember, change ch to sh, say and remember. Using whiteboards children write a number of words that rhyme with pin. Objectives Hear and say sounds in words in the order in which they occur Blend letters to read CVC words and recognize common digraphs Use their phonic knowledge to write simple regular words	Sand, water, handwriting trays and writing area resourced as on Monday. Objectives as before In pairs draw and paint large pictures of the characters from the story. These will be used as part of the display. Objectives Sustain attentive listening, responding to what they have heard by relevant comments, questions or actions Interact with others, negotiating plans and activities and taking turns in conversation Draw and label one of the characters from the film Objectives Attempt writing for various purposes Write their own names and simple text Use their phonic knowledge to write simple regular words and make phonetically plausible attempts at more complex words Guided reading	In pairs, using whiteboards, children write shin then write a number of words beginning with sh – ship, shop, shell, shed, she, – fish, dash, push, posh Objectives Hear and say sounds in words in the order in which they occur Use their phonic knowledge to write simple regular words Read some of the postcards the children have written in the writing area and show them a postcard written by the teacher Objective Attempt writing for various purposes, using features of different forms

	Whole-class work	Group activities	Plenary
Friday	Watch the film. Retell the story. Identify 6 key events. Use shared writing to model story board to record these 6 key events. Objectives Use talk to organize, sequence and clarify thinking, ideas, films and events Show an understanding of the elements of stories, such as main character, sequence of events, and openings Use language to imagine and re-create roles and stories Attempt writing for various purposes, using features of different forms	Explore and experiment with sounds, words and texts Show an understanding of the elements of stories, such as main character, sequence of events, and openings Writing area resourced as on Monday Objective Attempt writing for various purposes Draw and write a story board to retell the story of *The Lucky Dip* Objectives Show an understanding of the elements of stories, such as main character, sequence of events, and openings Attempt writing for various purposes, using features of different forms Use felt tips to write '*The Lucky Dip*' on strips of paper which will be used to frame the display. Objective Use a pencil and hold it effectively to form recognizable letters, most of which are correctly formed Play bingo with seaside words – ship, shell, fish, sea, bucket, spade, sand, mum, dad, girl, pin man, rabbit, bus, beach, swim Objectives Link sounds to letters, naming and sounding letters of the alphabet Blend letters to read CVC words and recognize common digraphs Read a range of familiar and common words and simple sentences Use story boxes to retell the story of *The Lucky Dip* Objectives Show an understanding of the elements of stories, such as main character, sequence of events, and openings Retell narratives in correct sequence, drawing on the language patterns of stories Use language to imagine and re-create roles and stories	Read and evaluate some storyboards. Correct some spellings using word bank or asking children Objectives Attempt writing for different purposes, using features of different forms Use their phonic knowledge to write simple regular words and make phonetically plausible attempts at more complex words

Week 2

	Whole-class work	Group activities	Plenary
Monday	Use one of the opening sentences from one child's story board as a starting point for expanding the writing. Use story language such as 'one day'. Include reference to the setting remind the children of the work they did on settings in the previous week. Model this using shared writing on the interactive white board. Complete this first section of the story which will be included in the wall story display. **Objectives** Show an understanding of the elements of stories, such as main character, sequence of events, and openings Retell narratives in the correct sequence, drawing on the language patterns of stories Attempt writing for various purposes, using features of different forms	Writing area resourced with postcards and writing implements **Objective** Attempt writing for various purposes ICT Postcard activity on the Fun with Spot website Attempt writing for various purposes Return to story board to add detail to the retelling of the story of *The Lucky Dip* **Objectives** Show an understanding of the elements of stories, such as main character, sequence of events, and openings Retell narratives in the correct sequence, drawing on the language patterns of stories Attempt writing for various purposes, using features of different forms Use felt tips to write '*The Lucky Dip*' on strips of paper which will be used to frame the display. **Objective** Use a pencil and hold it effectively to form recognizable letters, most of which are correctly formed Use story boxes to retell the story of *The Lucky Dip* **Objectives** Show an understanding of the elements of stories, such as main character, sequence of events, and openings Retell narratives in correct sequence, drawing on the language patterns of stories Use language to imagine and re-create roles and stories Guided writing Work with one group to complete section 2 of the story with added detail. Do this using shared writing. **Objectives** Show an understanding of the elements of stories, such as main character, sequence of events, and openings Retell narratives in the correct sequence, drawing on the language patterns of stories Attempt writing for various purposes, using features of different forms	Read the completed second section of the retelling completed in guided writing to the class. **Objectives** Show an understanding of the elements of stories, such as main character, sequence of events, and openings Retell narratives in the correct sequence, drawing on the language patterns of stories
Tuesday	Discuss the use of the role-play area which has been made into a cinema. What roles could the children take? What kinds of printed material could be found there? This can be made in the writing area. **Objectives** Use talk to organize, sequence and clarify thinking, ideas, feelings and events Use language to imagine and re-create roles and experiences	Use the cinema role-play area. **Objectives** Speak clearly and audibly with confidence and control and show awareness of the listener Extend their vocabulary, exploring the meanings and sounds of new words Interact with others, negotiating plans and activities and taking turns in conversation Use language to imagine and re-create roles and experiences Writing area resourced with material that can be used to produce resources for the role-play area **Objective**	Read the completed third section of the retelling completed in guided writing to the class. **Objectives** Show an understanding of the elements of stories, such as main character, sequence of events, and openings Retell narratives in the correct sequence, drawing on the language patterns of stories Discuss the use of the cinema role-play area. **Objective**

	Whole-class work	Group activities	Plenary
		Attempt writing for various purposes ICT Postcard activity on the Fun with Spot website Attempt writing for various purposes Return to story board to add detail to the retelling of the story of *The Lucky Dip* Objectives Show an understanding of the elements of stories, such as main character, sequence of events, and openings Retell narratives in the correct sequence, drawing on the language patterns of stories Attempt writing for various purposes, using features of different forms Use felt tips to write *The Lucky Dip* on strips of paper which will be used to frame the display. Objective Use a pencil and hold it effectively to form recognizable letters, most of which are correctly formed Use story boxes to retell the story of *The Lucky Dip* Objectives Show an understanding of the elements of stories, such as main character, sequence of events, and openings Retell narratives in correct sequence, drawing on the language patterns of stories Use language to imagine and re-create roles and stories Guided writing Work with one group to complete section 3 of the story with added detail. Do this using shared writing. Objectives Show an understanding of the elements of stories, such as main character, sequence of events, and openings Retell narratives in the correct sequence, drawing on the language patterns of stories Attempt writing for various purposes, using features of different forms	Sustain attentive listening, responding to what they have heard by relevant comments, questions or actions
Wednesday	Use one of the sections from one child's story board as a starting point for expanding the writing of the fourth section of the story. Use story language such as 'and then'. Include reference to characters' feelings and setting. Model this using shared writing on the interactive white board. Complete this fourth section of the story which will be included in the wall story display. Objectives Show an understanding of the elements of stories, such as main character, sequence of events, and openings Retell narratives in the correct sequence, drawing on the language patterns of stories Attempt writing for various purposes, using features of different	Use the cinema role-play area. Objectives Speak clearly and audibly with confidence and control and show awareness of the listener Extend their vocabulary, exploring the meanings and sounds of new words Interact with others, negotiating plans and activities and taking turns in conversation Use language to imagine and re-create roles and experiences ICT Postcard activity on the Fun with Spot website Attempt writing for various purposes Writing area resourced with material that can be used to produce resources for the role-play area Objective Attempt writing for various purposes	Read the completed fifth section of the retelling completed in guided writing to the class. Objectives Show an understanding of the elements of stories, such as main character, sequence of events, and openings Retell narratives in the correct sequence, drawing on the language patterns of stories Play the Lucky Dip Game Objectives Blend letters to read CVC words and recognize common digraphs Use their phonic knowledge to read simple regular words Read a range of familiar and common words independently

	Whole-class work	Group activities	Plenary
	forms	Return to story board to add detail to the retelling of the story of *The Lucky Dip* Objectives Show an understanding of the elements of stories, such as main character, sequence of events, and openings Retell narratives in the correct sequence, drawing on the language patterns of stories Attempt writing for various purposes, using features of different forms Use felt tips to write *The Lucky Dip* on strips of paper which will be used to frame the display. Objective Use a pencil and hold it effectively to form recognizable letters, most of which are correctly formed Use story boxes to retell the story of *The Lucky Dip* Objectives Show an understanding of the elements of stories, such as main character, sequence of events, and openings Retell narratives in correct sequence, drawing on the language patterns of stories Use language to imagine and re-create roles and stories Guided writing Work with one group to complete section 5 of the story with added detail. Do this using shared writing. Objectives Show an understanding of the elements of stories, such as main character, sequence of events, and openings Retell narratives in the correct sequence, drawing on the language patterns of stories Attempt writing for various purposes, using features of different forms	
Thursday	Introduce the digraph ea as in sea and beach. Ask the children to think of words that sound like sea. Write these on sticky notes. Look for common ways of making the long vowel e sound – ea, ee and ea and arrange these into two columns ee and ea Objectives Hear and say sounds in words in the order in which they occur Blend letters to read CVC words and recognize common digraphs	Use the cinema role-play area. Objectives Speak clearly and audibly with confidence and control and show awareness of the listener Extend their vocabulary, exploring the meanings and sounds of new words Interact with others, negotiating plans and activities and taking turns in conversation Use language to imagine and re-create roles and experiences Writing area resourced with material that can be used to produce resources for the role-play area Objective Attempt writing for various purposes Use felt tips to write 'The Lucky Dip' on strips of paper which will be used to frame the display. Objective Use a pencil and hold it effectively to form recognizable letters, most of which are correctly formed Use story boxes to retell the story of *The Lucky Dip* Objectives Show an understanding of the elements of stories, such as main character, sequence of events, and openings Retell narratives in correct sequence, drawing on the language patterns of stories	Read the completed final section of the retelling completed in guided writing to the class. Read the whole retelling together. Objectives Show an understanding of the elements of stories, such as main character, sequence of events, and openings Retell narratives in the correct sequence, drawing on the language patterns of stories

	Whole-class work	Group activities	Plenary
		Use language to imagine and re-create roles and stories Guided writing Work with one group to complete section 6 of the story with added detail. Do this using shared writing. Objectives Show an understanding of the elements of stories, such as main character, sequence of events, and openings Retell narratives in the correct sequence, drawing on the language patterns of stories Attempt writing for various purposes, using features of different forms Children make words containing long vowel e using play dough and letter cutters Objectives Hear and say sounds in words in the order in which they occur Use their phonic knowledge to write simple regular words	
Friday	Read the retelling of *The Lucky Dip* written by the children and the teacher together. Discuss the Lucy Dip. What did they like?, not like? Give reasons. Objectives Return to favourite books, songs, rhymes to be reread and enjoyed Listen with enjoyment, and respond to stories Use talk to organize, sequence and clarify thinking ideas, feelings and events Discuss what needs to be added to the display	Guided reading Objectives Explore and experiment with sounds, words and texts Show an understanding of the elements of stories, such as main character, sequence of events, and openings Complete painting objects for display. Children to work in pairs as far as possible. Objective Interact with others, negotiating plans and activities and taking turns in conversation Use the cinema role-play area. Objectives Speak clearly and audibly with confidence and control and show awareness of the listener Extend their vocabulary, exploring the meanings and sounds of new words Interact with others, negotiating plans and activities and taking turns in conversation Use language to imagine and re-create roles and experiences Writing area resourced with material that can be used to produce resources for the role-play area Objective Attempt writing for various purposes ICT Postcard activity on the Fun with Spot website Attempt writing for various purposes Use story boxes to retell the story of *The Lucky Dip* Objectives Show an understanding of the elements of stories, such as main character, sequence of events, and openings Retell narratives in correct sequence, drawing on the language patterns of stories Use language to imagine and re-create roles and stories Use phoneme spotter long vowel e story from Progression in Phonics supplement CD-ROM for phoneme spotter activity. Objectives Blend letters to read CVC words and recognize common digraphs	Using shared writing write the title and any other labels for the display of *The Lucky Dip* Objective Attempt writing for different purposes, using features of different forms

time and that the area changes during the course of the theme so that it continues to interest and stimulate the children. Figure 8.8 is an example of a planning sheet for a role-play area.

Activity

Think of a scenario for a role-play area in a nursery or reception class. This could be a setting related to a book such as *Cinderella* or a topic such as 'Toys'. Draw up a plan for the use of the area showing specific learning objectives and how the area will evolve over time. What preparatory work would you need to do with the children so that they made best use of the area? How could adults involve themselves in the children's play in order to develop it?

Routines

All settings and classes have established routines. Often these are linked to how the day begins, the ends of sessions, lunch or snack times and transition times between indoors and outdoors or between small and large group activities. These routines can contribute to children's learning if thought is given to how to make best use of them. For example, if children gather on the carpet after tidying and before going to outdoor play, they can look at books as they wait for their classmates. Alternatively, an adult can begin to say and sing some action rhymes with the children who have finished their tidying up. This often motivates those who are still talking or tidying. Sending children out to play can be done by using the initial letters of children's names, *All those with names that begin with B can put on their coats and go outside.* Children can help themselves to drinks and snacks but can record that they have done this by selecting their name card and placing it in the snack box. These are simple activities but can contribute to learning in communication, language and literacy.

Planning for bilingual learners

Universal experiences such as family life, eating, cooking, shopping or celebrating can vary across cultures and so teachers need to be sensitive to cultural differences and not assume that all children will have had the same experiences or the same understanding. It is important to find out about the cultural and family norms of the children in the class so that the planned curriculum is relevant to them all.

Although young bilingual learners will learn English as they take part in all the practical oral and written activities in nurseries and reception classes, it is

Role-Play Area: Supermarket

Roles	Checkout assistant, shelf stacker, manager, customers
Equipment and resources	Packages, clothes, newspapers, magazines, cards, shelving, till, table, carrier bags, money, baskets, café equipment
Literacy events	Make posters, make signs, order stock, restock shelves, read shopping lists, sign receipts, advertise for staff, burglary, sale and special offers, closing down sale
Introduction	Visit supermarket, observe contents and layout, interview staff about jobs and work in a supermarket model language and staff and customer behaviour
Learning intentions in communication, language and literacy	**Language for communication** Interact with others, negotiating plans and activities and taking turns in conversation **Writing** Attempt writing for different purposes, using features of different forms such as lists, stories and instructions Write their own names and other things such as labels and captions and begin to form simple sentences, sometimes using punctuation

Figure 8.8 *Example of a plan for a role-play area*

helpful to think about the language demands of some of the activities and books that are selected for teaching to make sure that these are suited to the children's level of development in English, as the following example shows.

Anton, a new entrant to the nursery, who had recently arrived in England from Portugal, was participating in an activity that was led by an adult. The teacher had a basket of socks, a washing line and some pegs. The children were asked to put the socks on the washing line in matched pairs. The key learning points were to talk about *same* and *different* and to recognize that two objects can make a pair. Anton willingly entered into the spirit of the activity selecting the socks that he liked and pegging them onto the line. However, none of the socks matched and Anton wanted to count all the socks that he had hung up. At this stage of Anton's English language development, the concepts of same, different and pair was too difficult for the practitioner to explain simply, and the vocabulary too difficult for Anton to understand in this context. He did use the word *socks* and was able to count to three.

Although the activity might have been cognitively appropriate the linguistic demands of the task made it too hard for Anton. The fact that he was completing the activity on his own added to his difficulties as he had no model to follow or help him to understand the adult's expectations. This episode is a reminder that the language associated with each activity needs to be carefully thought through. A list of new concepts and related target words can be made and entered onto the planning sheet. This can help practitioners to see if the activity will be too difficult or if key vocabulary needs to be introduced slowly and separately. Anton would probably have benefited from some preparatory activities introducing the words *same* and *different* and later the word *pair* before attempting the washing-line activity. He could have joined in with an activity where children were sorting pictures or objects using hoops labelled with the words *same* and *different*. An adult could have modelled the language asking questions such as, *Are these the same? Is this the same as … ? Does this go in the same hoop or the different hoop?*

Target vocabulary can be introduced in a variety of different ways in order to reinforce learning (Dodwell, 1999). For example, if the children are learning vocabulary associated with colours on one day, there could be:

- blue paint in the art area;
- blue collage materials;
- blue play dough;
- blue paper, pens and crayons in the writing area;
- blue lego bricks for construction;
- *The Blue Balloon* by Mick Inkpen (1989) for story time;
- blue water in the water tray; and
- the art and collage activities could be used to make a blue display.

Activity

Think of some activities which would have introduced Anton to the words and concepts of same, different and pair.

Planning for the deployment of adults

Adults are the most valuable resource for teaching and learning and so it is important that their time is well spent. It needs to be planned for, so that most of the time adults are working directly with groups and individuals. In the Foundation Stage adults can be:

- involved in play activities;

- leading activities;
- working with individuals;
- supervising the work of the whole class; and
- leading whole-class sessions.

During these times they can be doing many things, what Brailsford et al. (1999: 195) call 'the seven s's'. These are:

Supplying   Providing the resources necessary for children to develop their language and literacy skills.

Supporting   Helping children to achieve their aims by intervening sensitively when appropriate.

Scaffolding   Providing a framework for children so that they can achieve with help what they may be able to do on their own tomorrow.

Sharing   Sharing ideas, thoughts and experiences with children. Sharing books with children. Making literacy a social experience.

Showing   Providing a role model for children. Demonstrating ways of doing things.

Saying   Giving feedback to children on their language and literacy achievements. Helping them to develop the metacognitive skills necessary to analyse and discuss their own development.

Seeing   Observing children's development closely in order to plan effectively for their future development. Assessing their needs sensitively.

In all these ways adults help children to engage with activities and make the purposes for language and literacy clear. To make sure that all these aspects of teaching are catered for and groups and activities receive the help necessary for them to be successful, adults and their roles should be planned. For reference, the names of the adults who are responsible for particular activities or who are supporting individual children need to be indicated on the short-term plan. Adults do not always need to be overtly teaching in order for children to learn. They can teach by example and by joining in with children's activities, as the following example shows.

> One of the activities in the nursery was the free exploration of wet cornflour. One of the adults noticed that the children did not spend long with this activity and did not seem to be learning much from it. She went to sit at the wet cornflour table and began to make patterns. She vocalized her thoughts about what it felt like, how it changed if she tried to pick it up and about the patterns she was making. Some children sat down at the table and gradually began to imitate the adult. They talked

about the mixture using words such as *sticky, messy, cold, runny* and *hard*. The adult then began to draw letters in the cornflour saying the letters as she did so. Again the children followed suit and began to make some of the letters from their names. At no point did the adult try to directly teach the children, but her example encouraged the children to learn and talk about their learning. Her presence transformed the activity into a worthwhile learning experience.

The way in which teaching assistants are deployed in reception classes has received some criticism, particularly from Ofsted (2002). While they often work well with individuals, particularly when supporting children with special educational needs, they are sometimes underemployed during periods of whole-class teaching which is led by the class teacher. At these times they could be supporting individuals, working as a response partner with children to elicit language for thinking, observing named children or working in partnership with the teacher. Their time needs to be planned carefully so that children benefit as much as possible from the support that an additional adult can give.

Planning to meet individual needs

All those who work with young children are expected to provide for their diverse needs including the needs of children:

- with special educational needs;
- with disabilities;
- learning English as an additional language;
- who are more able; or
- who are of different ethnic groups including travellers, refugees and asylum seekers.

Practitioners need to identify and assess the children's needs and provide them with activities and support that enable their needs to be met and learning to take place.

When selecting themes and resources to use, care needs to be taken that the curriculum reflects the backgrounds of the children. For example, the books that are used should not just represent white, middle-class life; they should also reflect the multicultural nature of society. In addition, activities may need to be adapted. For example, story tapes and books in the children's home languages could be included in the listening area and the reading area. Some children will have learning programmes that have been devised by or with other professionals such as speech therapists or physiotherapists, and these programmes will need to be followed. A withdrawn child might benefit from playing and working with a friend whom he or she feels comfortable with, and adults might want to ensure that the two friends are called to an activity together. It might be necessary to allocate some small-group time to work with any children who are making better than average progress in communication, language and literacy to challenge them and extend their learning further.

Reviewing planning

Good planning underpins effective teaching and learning, and so plans may need to be adapted in order to improve either of these. The planning process is often described as a cycle with three elements: plan, implement and review. At the end of each day or each week it is good practice to review the teaching and learning that have occurred. Using information from observations, talking to children and feedback from all the staff, one could think about the following:

- Were the learning objectives appropriate to all the children?
- Do some children need more challenge?
- What did the children learn?
- Do some children need more experience but in a different way?
- Were all the children able to participate?
- Were the activities motivating and enjoyable?
- Were the activities at the right level?
- Did the activities contribute to the formation of positive dispositions as well as learning?
- Were the resources adequate?
- Were questioning and conversation used to support learning?

If some activities were not successful or if some children found the work too easy or too difficult, changes can be made in the next week's plans to ensure that the activities are more closely matched to the children's needs. Reviewing teaching and learning helps to make teaching and learning even more successful in the future. It is through continuously evaluating the quality of the children's learning and the progress that they are making that staff can assess whether their planning is meeting the children's changing needs. Some practitioners include an evaluation column on the short-term planning sheet and note down information about the activities and the children's learning so that the next week's planning can be adapted. Figure 8.9 shows an example of this.

Theme 'Storytelling' based on *Rosie's Walk* by Pat Hutchins   Week 1

	Monday	Tuesday	Wednesday	Thursday	Friday	Evaluation and implications for planning
Sand tray	Resource the sand tray with farm animals and props to encourage the children to play with the story. Learning objectives *Language for Thinking Green: Begin to use talk to pretend imaginary situations* *Language for Thinking Grey: Use language to imagine and re-create roles and experiences*			Resource the sand tray with farm animals and props to encourage the children to play with the story. Learning objectives *Language for Thinking Green: Begin to use talk to pretend imaginary situations* *Language for Thinking Grey: Use language to imagine and re-create roles and experiences*		Some children did not use *Rosie's Walk* as a prompt for their play. They created their own stories. Demonstrate the use of this resource next week or make sure an adult plays alongside the children and models what is expected.
Writing area			Make repeating patterns using single letters, e.g. a row of hhhhh Some of these can be used to decorate the class book in week 3. Learning objectives *Handwriting Green: Begin to form recognizable letters* *Handwriting Grey: Use a pencil and hold it effectively to form recognizable letters, most of which are correctly formed*			Many children need need more practice at this. Encourage more children to use the cornflour activity and perhaps substitute a shallow sand tray letter formation activity for the cornflour next week. Adam, Tanya and Will found this very difficult. Provide some alternative and additional handwriting activities for them. Will has an awkward pencil grip. Help him to find a more comfortable way of holding a pencil.

Figure 8.9 *Plan showing weekly review of activities and learning*

Conclusion

Careful planning is the key to successful learning and teaching. It ensures that children are learning and that they are making progress in their learning. Although learning objectives may be set out in official documents and guidelines, practitioners have the freedom to teach these in ways that are appropriate to the needs and ages of the children they work with and in ways that will motivate and stimulate children.

 Further reading

Tassoni, P. and Hucker, K. (2000) *Planning Play and the Early Years*. Oxford: Heinemann.

This book provides practical guidance on how to plan a practical and play-based curriculum for young children. It also contains sections on the value of play and examines different approaches to planning in general.

References

Allen, P. (1982) *Who Sank the Boat?* London: Puffin Books.

Anning, A. and Edwards, A. (2006) *Promoting Children's Learning from Birth to Five: Developing the New Early Years Professional.* 2nd edn. Maidenhead: Open University Press.

Bang, M. (1987) *Ten, Nine, Eight.* London: Red Fox.

Beard, R. (1998) *National Literacy Strategy: Review of Research and Other Related Evidence.* London: DfEE.

bfi education (2003a) *Look Again!* London: British Film Institute.

bfi education (2003b) *Starting Stories: A Film and Literacy Resource for Three to Seven Year Olds.* London: British Film Institute.

Black, P. and William, D. (1998) *Inside the Black Box: Raising Standards through Classroom Assessment.* London: School of Education, King's College.

Brailsford, M., Hetherington, D. and Abram, E. (1999) 'Desirable planning for language and literacy', in J. Marsh and E. Hallet (eds), *Desirable Literacies: Approaches to Language and Literacy in the Early Years.* London: Paul Chapman Publishing. pp. 191–213.

Bromley, H. (2000) *Book-based Reading Games.* London: CLPE.

Bromley, H. (2003) 'Playing with the literacy hour', *The Primary English Magazine*, 9(5): 8–11.

Browne, E. (1994) *Handa's Surprise.* London: Walker Books.

Browne, P. (1995) *African Animals ABC.* London: Barefoot Books.

Bruce, T. (ed.) (2006) *Early Childhood – A Guide for Students.* London: Sage.

Bruner, J. (1980) *Under Five in Britain.* London: Grant McIntyre.

Bruner, J. (1986) *Actual Minds, Possible Worlds.* Cambridge, MA: Harvard University Press.

Burningham, J. (1977) *Come away from the water, Shirley.* London: Jonathan Cape.

Burningham, J. (1978) *Mr Gumpy's Outing.* London: Puffin Books.

Burningham, J. (1980) *The Shopping Basket.* London: Jonathan Cape.

Butler, D. (1979) *Cushla and Her Books*. London: Hodder & Stoughton.

Butterworth, N. and Inkpen, M. (1992) *Jasper's Beanstalk*. London: Hodder & Stoughton.

Cambourne, B. (1988) *The Whole Story: Natural Learning and the Acquisition of Learning in the Classroom*. Gosford, NSW: Ashton Scholastic.

Campbell, R. (1984) *Dear Zoo*. London: Puffin Books.

Carle, E. (1997) *The Tiny Seed*. London: Puffin Books.

Clarke, S. (2003) *Enriching Feedback in the Primary Classroom: Oral and Written Feedback from Teachers and Children*. London: Hodder & Stoughton.

Clay, M.M. (1975) *What Did I Write?* London: Heinemann.

Clay, M.M. (1985) *The Early Detection of Reading Difficulties: A Diagnostic Survey with Recovery Procedures*. 3rd edn. Portsmouth, NH: Heinemann.

Cook, A. (1998) *The Wheels on the Bus*. London: Walker Books.

Cousins, J. (1990) 'Are your little humpty dumpties floating or sinking?', *Early Years*, 10(2): 28–38.

Cousins, L. (2002) *Maisy at the Beach*. London: Walker Books.

Crystal, D. (1997) *The Cambridge Encyclopaedia of Language*. 2nd edn. Cambridge: Cambridge University Press.

Cummins, J. (2000) *Language Power and Pedagogy: Bilingual Children in the Crossfire*. Clevedon: Multilingual Matters.

Dale, P. (1987) *Bet you can't!* London: Walker Books.

Deafness Research UK (2005) Facts and figures about deafness in the UK, www.deafnessresearch.org.uk/did+you+know+page1888.html, accessed 3 July 2006.

Desforges, C. and Abouchaar, A. (2003) *The Impact of Parental Involvement, Parental Support and Family Education on Pupil Achievement and Adjustment: A Literature Review*. DfES research report 433, 2003. London: DfES.

Department for Education and Employment (DfEE) (2001) *Developing Early Writing*. London: DfEE.

Department for Education and Employment/Qualifications and Curriculum Authority (DfEE/QCA) (1999) *The National Curriculum: Handbook for Primary Teachers in England*. London: DfEE.

Department for Education and Skills (DfES) (2001a) *National Literacy Strategy: Framework for Teaching*. London: DfES.

Department for Education and Skills (DfES) (2001b) *Progression in Phonics*. London: DfES.

Department for Education and Skills (DfES) (2001c) *Special Educational Needs and Disability Discrimination Act 2001*. London: HMSO.

Department for Education and Skills (DfES) (2001d) *Special Educational Needs Code of Practice*. London: DfES.

Department for Education and Skills (DfES) (2002) *The National Literacy and Numeracy Strategies: Including All Children in the Literacy Hour and the Daily Mathematics Session*. London: DfES.

Department for Education and Skills (DfES) (2003) *Excellence and Enjoyment: A Strategy for Primary Schools*. London: DfES.

Department for Education and Skills (DfES) (2004a) *Every Child Matters: The Next Steps*. Green Paper. London: HMSO.

Department for Education and Skills (DfES) (2004b) *Playing with Sounds: A Supplement to Progression in Phonics*. London: DfES.

Department for Education and Skills (DfES) (2004c) *Removing Barriers to Achievement: The Government's Strategy for SEN*. Nottingham: DfES.

Department of Education and Science (DES) (1975) *A Language for Life* (Bullock Report). London: HMSO.

Dodd, L. (1985) *Hairy Maclary from Donaldson's Dairy*. London: Puffin Books.

Dodwell, E. (1999) '"I can tell lots of Punjabi": developing language and literacy with bilingual children', in J. Marsh and E. Hallett (eds), *Desirable Literacies: Approaches to Language and Literacy in the Early Years*. London: Paul Chapman Publishing. pp. 17–33.

Edgington, M. (2004) *The Foundation Stage Teacher in Action: Teaching 3, 4 and 5 Year Olds*. 3rd edn. London: Paul Chapman Publishing.

Edwards, A. and Warin, J. (1999) 'Parental involvement in raising the achievement of primary school pupils: why bother?', *Oxford Review of Education*, 25(3): 325–41.

Edwards, V. (2004) *The Other Languages: A Guide to Multilingual Classrooms*. Reading: National Centre for Language and Literacy.

Effective Provision of Pre-school Education (EPPE) project, www.ioe.ac.uk/projects/eppe, accessed 23 July 2006.

Ehlert, L. (1993) *Eating the Alphabet: Fruit and Vegetables from A to Z*. London: Orion.

Ellis, S. and Barrs, M. (1996) *The Core Book*. London: CLPE.

Ferreiro, E. and Teberosky, A. (1982) *Literacy before Schooling*. Portsmouth, NH: Heinemann.

Frith, U. (1985) 'Developmental dyslexia', in K.E. Patterson, M. Coltheart and J.C. Marshall (eds), *Surface Dyslexia*. Hove: Lawrence Erlbaum Associates.

Gentry, J.R. (1982) 'An analysis of developmental spelling in GNYS AT WRK', *The Reading Teacher*, 36: 192–200.

Geraghty, P. (1994) *The Hunter*. London: Red Fox.

Gillen, J., with Stone, L. and Cosier, L. (2001) '"Is that the little pig?" – using toy telephones in the early years classroom', in P. Goodwin (ed.), *The Articulate Classroom: Talking and Learning in the Primary School*. London: David Fulton. pp. 93–100.

Goodwin, P. (ed.) (2001) *The Articulate Classroom: Talking and Learning in the Primary School*. London: David Fulton.

Goswami, U. (1999) 'Phonological development and reading by analogy: epilinguistic and metalinguistic issues', in J. Oakhill and R. Beard (eds), *Reading Development and the Teaching of Reading: A Psychological Perspective*. Oxford: Blackwell.

Griffiths, N. (2001) Storysacks. Reading: Reading and Language Information Centre

Guppy, P. and Hughes. M. (1999) *The Development of Independent Reading*. Buckingham: Open University Press.

Hall, N. (1999) 'The struggle to punctuate: a case study of two children learning', in P. Goodwin (ed.), *The Literate Classroom*. London: David Fulton.

Hall, N. and Robinson, A. (1995) *Exploring Writing and Play in the Early Years*. London: David Fulton.

Harste, J.C., Woodward, V.A. and Burke, C.L. (1984) *Language Stories and Literacy Lessons*. Portsmouth, NH: Heinemann.

Heap, S. and Sharratt, N. (2004) *Red Rockets and Rainbow Jelly*. London: Puffin Books.

Heenan, J. (1986) *Writing: Process and Product*. Auckland: Longman Paul.

Her Majesty's Inspectorate (HMI) (2004) *Reading for Purpose and Pleasure: An Evaluation of the Teaching of Reading in Primary Schools*. London: Ofsted.

Hiebert, E. and Raphael, T. (1998) *Early Literacy Instruction*. Fort Worth, TX: Harcourt Brace.

Hill, E. (1980) *Where's Spot?* London: Puffin Books.

Hissey, J. (1994) *Old Bear*. London: Red Fox.

Hornby, G. (2000) *Improving Parental Involvement*. London: Cassell.

Hughes, S. (2005) *Out and About throughout the Year*. London: Walker Books.

Hutchins, P. (1970) *Rosie's Walk*. London: The Bodley Head.

Hutchins, P. (1972) *Titch*. London: Puffin Books.

Hutchins, P. (1986) *The Doorbell Rang*. London: Puffin Books.

Inkpen, M. (1989) *The Blue Balloon*. London: Hodder & Stoughton.

Katz, L. and Chard, S. (1989) *Engaging Children's Minds: The Project Approach*. Norwood, NJ: Ablex.

Lancaster, L. (2003) 'Moving into literacy: how it all begins', in N. Hall, J. Larson and J. Marsh (eds), *Handbook of Childhood Literacy*. London: Sage. pp. 145–53.

Lancome, J. (1998) *Walking through the Jungle*. London: Walker Books.

Lewis, M. and Fisher, R. (2003) *Curiosity Kits*. Reading: National Centre for Language and Literacy.

Marsh, J. (2004) 'The techno-literacy practices of young children', Journal *of Early Childhood Research*, 2(1): 51–66.

Marsh, J. (2005) 'Digikids: young children, popular culture and media', in N. Yelland (ed.), *Critical Issues in Early Childhood Education*. Buckingham: Open University Press. pp. 181–96.

Martin, D. (2000) *Teaching Children with Speech and Language Difficulties*. London: David Fulton.

McNaughton, C. (1996) *Suddenly!* London: Picture Lions.

Millard, E. (2003) 'Gender and early childhood literacy', in N. Hall, J. Larson and J. Marsh (eds), *Handbook of Early Childhood Literacy*. London: Sage Publications. pp. 22–33.

Miller, L. (1999) *Moving towards Literacy with Environmental Print*. Royston, Herts: UKRA.

Moore, I. (1990) *Six Dinner Sid*. London: Walker Books.

Mortimer, H. (2001) *Special Needs and Early Years Provision*. London: Continuum.

Moyles, J. (1989) *Just Playing?* Buckingham: Open University Press.

Murphy, J. (1983) *Whatever Next!* London: Macmillan.

O'Sullivan, O. and Thomas, A. (2000) *Understanding Spelling*. London: CLPE.

Office for Standards in Education (Ofsted) (2002) 'Teaching assistants in primary schools: an evaluation of the quality and impact of their work', www.ofsted.gov.uk, accessed 5 May 2006

Paley, V.G. (1981) *Wally's Stories*. London: Harvard University Press.

Prater, J. (1993) *Once upon a time*. London: Walker Books

Piaget, J. (1951) *Play, Dreams and Imitation in Childhood*. London: Routledge and Kegan Paul.

Pfister, M. (1996) *The Rainbow Fish*. London: North–South Books.

Porter, L. (2002) *Educating Young Children with Special Educational Needs*. London: Paul Chapman Publishing.

Primary National Strategy (PNS) (2004) *The Literacy Planning CD-ROM*. London: DfES.

Primary National Strategy (PNS) (2005) *Boys' Writing Flyers*. London: DfES.

Primary National Strategy (PNS) (2006) *Draft Framework for Teaching Literacy: Consultation Document*. London: DfES.

Qualifications and Curriculum Authority (QCA) (2000a) *A Language in Common: Assessing English as an Additional Language*. London: QCA.

Qualifications and Curriculum Authority (QCA) (2000b) *Curriculum Guidance for the Foundation Stage*. London: QCA.

Qualifications and Curriculum Authority (QCA) (2001) *Planning for Learning in the Foundation Stage*. London: QCA.

Qualifications and Curriculum Authority (QCA) (2003) *Foundation Stage Profile Handbook*. London: QCA.

Rose, J. (2006) *Independent Review of the Teaching of Early Reading: Final Report*. London: DfES.

Rosen, M. (1989) *We're going on a bear hunt!* London: Walker Books.

Roskos, K. and Neuman, S. (1993) 'Descriptive observations of adults' facilitation of literacy in young children's play', *Early Childhood Research Quarterly*, 8(1): 77–97.

Sammons, P., Taggart, B., Smees, R., Sylva, K., Melhuish, E., Siraj-Blatchford, I. and Elliot, K. (2003) *The Early Years Transition and Special Educational Needs (EYTSEN) Project*. Nottingham: DfES.

Sanders, D., White, G., Burge, B., Sharp, C., Eames, A., McEune, R. and Grayson, H. (2005) *A Study of the Transition from the Foundation Stage to Key Stage 1*. DfES Research Report SSU/2005/FR/013. London: DfES.

Sassoon, R. (2003) *Handwriting: The Way to Teach It.* 2nd edn. London: Paul Chapman Publishing.

Sharp, E. (2005) *Learning through Talk in the Early Years: Practical Activities for the Classroom.* London: Paul Chapman Publishing.

Sharratt, N. (1992) *The Green Queen.* London: Walker Books.

Sheldon, D. (1988) *I Forgot.* London: Walker Books.

Smidt, S. (2002) *A Guide to Early Years Practice.* 2nd edn. Abingdon: Routledge/Falmer.

Smilansky, S. (1968) *The Effects of Socio-Dramatic Play on Disadvantaged Preschool Children.* New York: John Wiley.

Smith, F. (1982) *Writing and the Writer.* Portsmouth, NH: Heinemann.

Smith, F. (1994) *Understanding Reading.* 5th edn. Hillsdale, NJ: Lawrence Erlbaum Associates.

Solity, J. (2002) 'Reading schemes versus "real books" revisited', *Literacy Today,* 31, www.literacytrust.org.uk/Pubs/solity.html, accessed 23 March 2006.

Solity, J. (2006) Real Books are Alive and Well, Paper presented to the January 2006 Educational and Child Psychology Annual Conference, Bournemouth.

Sutherland, M. (2005) *Gifted and Talented in the Early Years.* London: Paul Chapman Publishing.

Tassoni, P. (2003) *Supporting Special Needs: Understanding Inclusion in the Early Years.* Oxford: Heinemann Educational.

Tassoni, P. and Hucker, K. (2000) *Planning Play and the Early Years.* Oxford: Heinemann.

Tizard, B. and Hughes, M. (2002) *Young Children Learning.* 2nd edn. Oxford: Blackwell.

Tucker, N. (2002) *The Rough Guide to Children's Books 0–5.* London: Rough Guides/Penguin.

Vygotsky, L.S. (1986) *Thought and Language.* Cambridge, MA: MIT Press.

Wade, B. and Moore, M (1993) *Bookstart in Birmingham: A Description and Evaluation of an Exploratory British Project to Encourage Sharing Books with Babies. Book Trust Report 2.* London: Bookstart.

Wade, B. and Moore, M. (2000) 'A sure start with books', *Early Years,* 20(2): 39–46.

Watanabe, S. (1977) *How do I put it on?* London: Puffin Books.

Weinberger, J. (1996) *Literacy Goes to School.* London: Paul Chapman Publishing.

Whitehead, M. (2002) *Developing Language and Literacy with Young Children.* 2nd edn. London: Paul Chapman Publishing.

Williams, S. (2001) 'A bridge too far? How Biff, Chip, Kipper and Floppy fail the apprentice reader', *English in Education,* 32(2): 12–24.

Wolfendale, S. (2000) 'Effective schools for the future: incorporating the parental and family dimension', in S. Wolfendale and J. Bastiani (eds), *The Contribution of Parents to School Effectiveness.* London: David Fulton. pp. 1–18.

Wolfendale, S. and Bastiani, J. (eds) (2000) *The Contribution of Parents to School Effectiveness*. London: David Fulton.

Wood, D. (1988) *How Children Think and Learn: The Social Contexts of Cognitive Development*. Oxford: Blackwell.

Wood, D. and Bennett, N. (1999) 'Progression and continuity in early childhood education: tensions and contradictions', *International Journal of Early Years Education*, 7(1): 5–16.

Younger, M. and Warrington, M., with Gray, J., Ruddock, J., McLellan, R., Bearne, E., Kershner, R. and Bricheno, P. (2005) *Raising Boys' Achievement*. Nottingham: DfES.

Teaching and learning communication, language and learningTeaching and learning communication, language and learning

Index